D0229130

Oxford University Press, Walton Street, Oxford OX2 6DP

Oxford London
New York Toronto Melbourne Auckland
Kuala Lumpur Singapore Hong Kong Tokyo
Delhi Bombay Calcutta Madras Karachi
Nairobi Dar es Salaam Cape Town

and associated companies in
Beirut Berlin Ibadan Mexico City Nicosia

Oxford is a trade mark of Oxford University Press

First published 1985

British Library Cataloguing in Publication Data
Moffat, William
A History of Scotland.
Bk. 1
1. Scotland – History
I. Title II. Drury, Neil
941.1 DA762
ISBN 0-19-917053-3

A History of Scotland		**Hardback**	**Paperback**
Book 1	*Earliest times to the last of the Celtic kings*	0 19 917053 3	0 19 917042 8
Book 2	*The Normans to the House of the High Steward*	0 19 917054 1	0 19 917043 6
Book 3	*James I to Restoration*	0 19 917055 X	0 19 917044 4
Book 4	*The Restoration to the Victorians*	0 19 917056 8	0 19 917051 7
Book 5	*Modern Times*	0 19 917064 9	0 19 917063 0

Phototypeset by Tradespools Ltd., Frome, Somerset
Printed in Hong Kong

Contents

The Long Thaw

Fifteen thousand years ago the world was locked in the freezing grip of an ice age. The whole of northern Europe, including almost all the land which is now Britain, lay covered by a vast ice sheet.

Where the ice ended, great tundra plains stretched wide and far to the horizon. Only a few shrubs and stunted trees showed above the mosses and grasses which provided grazing for bison, horse and reindeer. Swept by blizzards in the winter and scoured by dust storms in the summer it was a hard and difficult place for man to live. But the hunting was good and there were caves for shelter. People adapted and survived.

But already great changes were taking place. Changes so important that they would alter the whole course of mankind; changes so slow that they would not be noticed even in a lifetime. The long thaw had begun.

above: Polar ice-cap
below left: Britain and north-west Europe fifteen thousand years ago
below right: Britain and north-west Europe ten thousand years ago

The ice melts

For five thousand years the edge of the ice crept back. Huge quantities of water poured into the oceans as the ice melted and the land was uncovered. In the warmer conditions that followed trees grew in abundance and the open plains of Europe were slowly covered by dark and brooding forests. Ancient Scotland was a land of mountains and woods through which rivers made their straggling way to the sea. Oak, ash and elm filled the lowland valleys. Further north, the hardier birch, rowan and pine crowded the upland forests.

In the thickly overgrown valleys prowling wolves and bears sheltered. Above the tree-line rose the forbidding expanses of the higher slopes. And where the land was flatter in desolate moors, dense scrub gave way only to marsh and reedy loch.

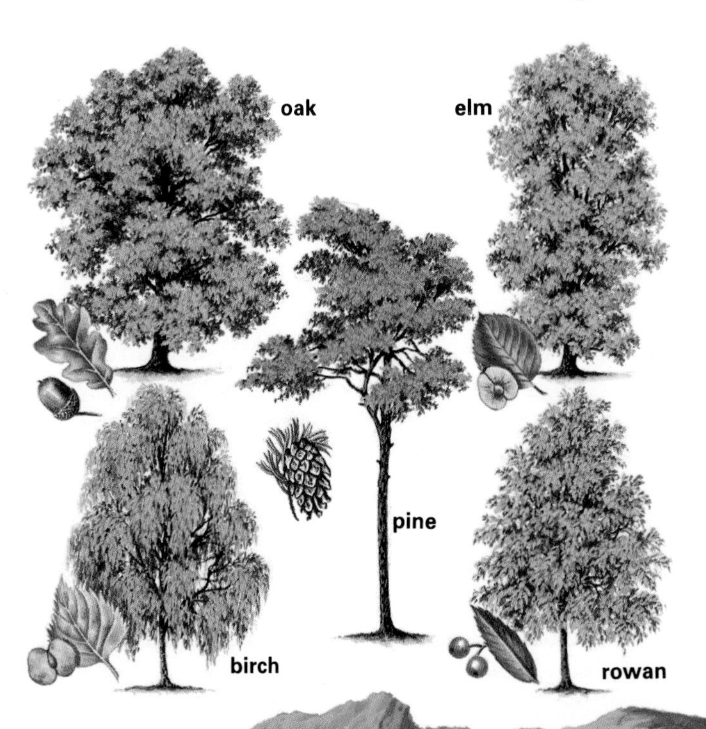

The hunters arrive

North to this land people came to hunt. They came in small groups, men and women, girls and boys, who suffered and enjoyed life just as we do today. At any one time there may have been no more than seventy human beings in the whole of Scotland. Man was a rare species eight thousand years ago.

For two thousand years the small hunting bands made their way from south Britain. They would stop for a week or so, perhaps for a whole season, when the hunting was good, and they left their mark. The map shows a place in North Fife now called Morton farm. The stone tools and weapons, bones and shells, refuse and ashes found there proclaim the presence, thousands of years ago, of Scotland's first known inhabitants.

Men lived as hunters, eating the meat of red deer and roe deer, wild boar and wild ox, of grouse, black-cock and capercaillie. With fishtraps they caught large cod. They gathered shellfish and wild fruit and cut the flesh from the carcases of stranded Blue Whales and Grey Seals.

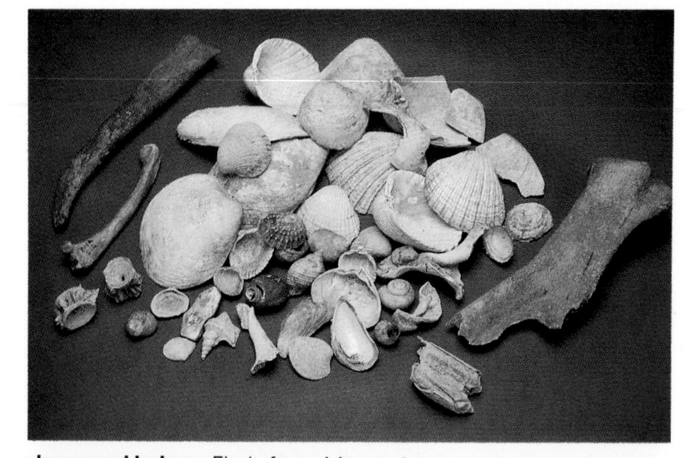

above and below: Finds from Morton farm

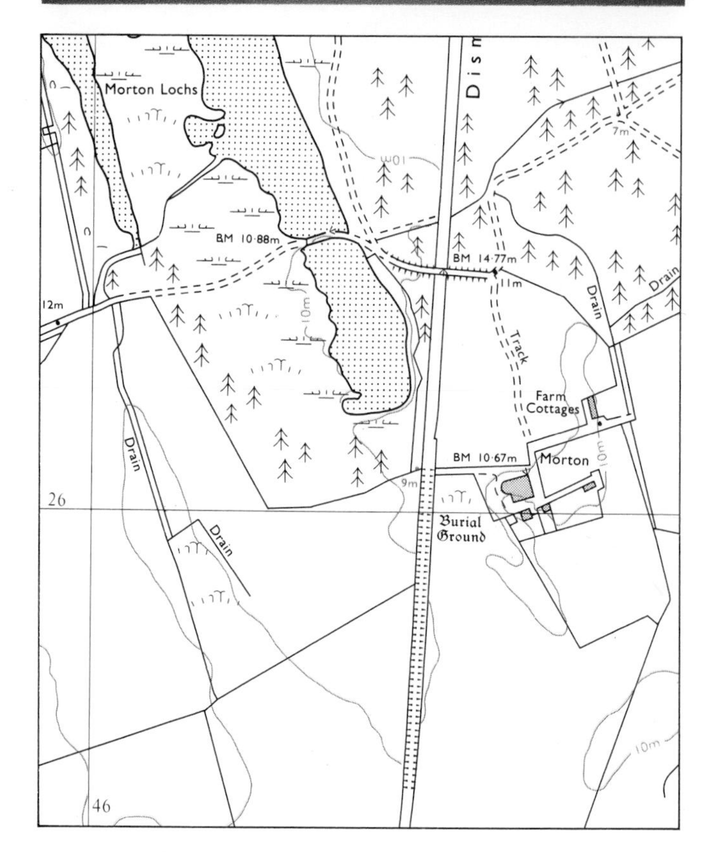

red deer

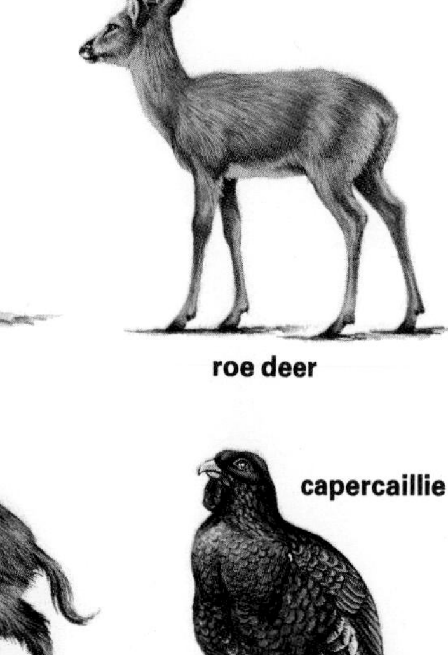

roe deer

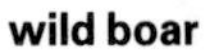

wild boar

capercaillie

wild ox

They found shelter in cave mouths or constructed windbreaks and 'tents' by driving stakes into the ground and covering them with hides. But they did not settle. Scotland's earliest population moved through the forest in pursuit of game. Because they had found no other way to provide food they were obliged to follow the food trail, unable to settle long enough to form the larger communities in which civilization could be nurtured.

Stone Age farmers

The animals which, for thousands of years, had roamed the tundra as man's natural prey could not live in the huge forests that gradually swallowed up the plains of Europe. Gone now were the great herds of bison and reindeer. Gone too were the mammoths. The life support system was changing and man would have to adapt or perish. The hunter must learn to become a farmer.

Animals and crops

The ancient hunters were no less clever than we are to-day and they already knew how to tame animals. This had been learned when dogs were first trained to help in the hunt. Now, if the hunters could no longer pursue the great herds over open country, as their forefathers had done, they would keep the animals close by. They would tame them as once their dogs had been tamed.

It was natural enough for hunters to find a way of getting meat. But they had also been in the habit of gathering wild plants to eat. Perhaps the plants too could be tamed and grown at home. And so the ideas of raising crops and rearing animals were born – though not necessarily together. Even today the two types of farming may be carried out separately.

Where and when it all began is not known. By the time the first hunters arrived in Scotland, people in Iraq were already growing wheat and keeping animals. But what these early farmers could not have realized was that more, much more, would happen than a simple change from hunting to farming. Though people still hunted and fished they were no longer *forced* to wander the food trails of Europe. Now they could settle down and live in communities. It would take a few thousand years to arrange, of course, but nothing would ever be quite the same again.

The farmers arrive

Through the centuries the early farmers spread out over Europe until they had reached the north-western coast about six thousand years ago. Then, perhaps late one summer when the grain was safely harvested, some of these farmers and herdsmen put to sea in their sturdy little boats. With them were their families and their means of living – animals for rearing and seed corn for planting. In the brightness of that distant morning they had forsaken their old homelands in search of somewhere new to live. The wanderlust of the hunter lived on in the heart of the new farmer. In time they reached the northern place that, one far off day, would be Scotland. There they settled to raise their crops and tend their beasts, sharing the land with the hunters who had come before them.

A place to live

Even to the hardiest adventurers this wet and windy country, choked with the darkest densest woodland, must have seemed a daunting place. But the early farmers had brought a weapon to fight the forest – a polished blade of hard stone set firmly on a strong wooden shaft. Throughout history Scotland would ring to the sound of the woodman's axe.

They had their boats too. Overland travel at that time was almost impossible. The new arrivals would find that their best way of getting about was on the rivers that straggled and twisted through marshes thick with alder and willow. Our first roads were waterways.

Year upon year, generation upon generation, the farmers pressed home their counter attack on the forest. Families who spent their lives in a world of trees naturally built their houses of timber. Unfortunately, in time, the timbers rotted leaving little or no trace of the houses once filled with the noise and bustle of home. Very little indeed would be known about the day to day living of these early people had not some of them chosen to settle in the northern Isles of Orkney.

modern wheat and barley

The early farmers would first find themselves a likely place to settle, often at a river mouth. With their stone axes they would hack at the solid mass of trees and undergrowth until a clearing was made. They burned the timber and brushwood not required for building or fuel. They raked ash from the fires into the ground with wooden digging sticks or hoes to improve the quality of the seed bed. On this fertile bed they planted their seeds. They raised crops of wheat and sometimes barley. The flocks of sheep and herds of cattle and goats grazed on the rough grass and tree foliage. After ten years or so the soil would become exhausted through overuse. Then they would find a new place and begin all over again.

ancient wheat and barley

Skara Brae

More than four thousand years ago a small group of farmers took their families and sailed north from Scotland. For twenty or so miles they sailed, before beaching their boats on the western shore of the Orkney Island now called Mainland. That day the weather would have been fair. It is most unlikely that they would have put to sea otherwise. For men who had experienced the struggle of forest life, the almost treeless landscape of that island, peacefully set against a blue sky, must have seemed a most welcome sight. If so, they had reckoned without the reason that trees grow so sparingly on Orkney. For many days of the year howling winds rage down Eyehollow Sound, scouring the earth and tearing at all that stands in their path.

Feeble leather tents or flimsy timber shelters would not long bear the weight of the great winds. They chose the place known today as Skara Brae, overlooking the beautiful Bay of Skail, and dug themselves in. To be more correct it was their houses that were dug in. They built down into the sand, lining the walls and the floors with drystone slabs. Where timber was scarce it was natural to use stone. And there they settled tending their flocks and herds, fishing and gathering shells perhaps for bait, occasionally hunting the red deer.

The ten houses, which had been hidden by the deep sand for thousands of years, were laid bare once more, by the savage winter gales of 1850. The remains of a meal were found by a bedside and in a passage a string of beads lay where it had fallen when Skara Brae was abandoned about 1500 BC. Tools too and other things of value were still there in the fully furnished homes of Orkney's stone age farmers.

Because the Orkney settlers' homes were built of stone they did not perish with the passing of time. The builders were of the same stock as the farmers who cut clearings in the mainland forests and whose timber houses have not survived to be seen today. Skara Brae shows how these early families adapted their ideas to suit the bare windswept landscape of Orkney and, in so doing, tells us a great deal about how they lived in the dense woodland of Scotland.

Houses

Each house was about as big as a good sized modern living room. It was joined to the others by sunken passageways, lined in stone. The whole domestic complex was roofed over with turfs supported on driftwood beams, or perhaps whalebones. Even the furniture was of stone and included a dresser not unlike the wooden ones still used in farmhouse kitchens today. On each side of the door were bed recesses, filled with soft springy heather. Cupboards were let into the thickness of the walls. The peat fire burned in a square hearth set in the centre of the floor. The smoke found an outlet through a hole in the roof. To the side, slab-lined boxes sunk in the floor, contained seafood and live bait, and fresh water supplies. When the archaeologists were digging at the site in 1928 they hired a 'housekeeper' to cook and clean for the team. She moved into one of the little stone dwellings and lived there comfortably, a modern tenant of a house built more than four thousand years before.

Problems

Sometimes things went wrong. The crops failed. The animals sickened. And nothing the farmer could do would make any difference. There must have been times when these early people felt that nature gave with one hand only to snatch it all away again with the other. Flood, tempest, frost and drought taught man stern lessons. To these first farmers, it must have seemed that there were great powers far beyond their understanding with which they would be wise to make their peace.

They buried their dead with ceremony and ritual, perhaps with such mysterious forces in mind. Just nine miles from Skara Brae is the magnificent tomb at Maeshowe, finely engineered in cut stone. Maeshowe was a major project far beyond the labour force of a single family group. These ancient herdsmen and farmers built other ceremonial monuments too, of great size and difficulty like the mighty Stonehenge near Salisbury in England, monuments requiring proper design and planning, large workparties and good organization, and time in which to build.

top: Tomb at Maeshowe
above left: The Skara Brae site today
below left: Map showing sites of axe factories.

The first traders

These early farmers started trade too and some industrial enterprise. And all this was because of their axes. The kind of stone which made the best axe blades could not be picked up just anywhere. So when a good supply of the right stone was found on Creag-na-Caillich near Killin in Perthshire, people set up an axe factory, sending their finished blades to the North East, where Aberdeenshire now lies. Nobody knows exactly how this trading was carried out. Perhaps they exchanged axe heads for useful things like food or seed, hides or pottery.

They really did manage to do quite a lot, these stone age farmers who first came to Scotland. They introduced cattle, sheep and goats; they brought wheat and barley too. They made boats that were seaworthy, sledges for snow or smooth ground and, most important of all, they brought the tool which cleared a living space for mankind – the woodman's axe.

These axe-heads are made from highly polished Jadeite, and though useless, were much prized by their owners.

Men of Bronze

A new craft

For four thousand years or more, people struggled for survival in this northern land, using tools and weapons of stone. This was our Stone Age, so called because stone was the best material people could find for making a sharp edge – the tip of the hunter's arrow, the blade of the woodman's axe. But in other parts of the world, change was afoot. New and better materials had been discovered. A new craft had been invented. Even as our first farmers tilled the soil and tended their animals, people skilled in this new craft were on the move. They travelled westwards across the plains of north Europe bringing with them tools and weapons, superior to those of stone. What is even more important they brought also the secret ways by which the new materials could be found and worked and finished. They could extract metals from the earth and shape them to man's purpose, copper and bronze for their tools and weapons, gold for ornament.

The newcomers

By about 2000 BC these men of bronze with their families had reached Scotland. They had sailed across the North Sea to find new homes. With them they had brought what supplies and livestock they could carry in their small boats. Along Scotland's eastern shore they had searched out the natural harbours formed at the mouths of rivers, there to shelter and there to enter their new homeland upon a great adventure. Many of them chose to settle in the Valleys of the Dee and the Don in the north-east. They had arrived in Scotland at the very place where the great city of Aberdeen now stands. They had found a river-mouth haven which would continue to give shelter to seafarers right up to the present time. To-day it serves the country's greatest new industry – oil, just as four thousand years ago it was the gateway for the great new industry of metalwork. Aberdeen, which means simply the mouth of the Dee, has been a port for a very long time indeed.

Like the Stone Age farmers who had come before them, the newcomers cut clearings in the great forests. With simple wooden hoes they tilled the soil and raised crops of barley which they preferred to wheat. They tended their sheep and cattle, goats and pigs. They made attractive pottery. Those amongst them who possessed the secrets of the new metal craft prepared their special fires. Layers of charcoal and ore were enclosed in a clay and stone furnace. Blasts of air forced the fire to burn so hotly that molten metal trickled to the bottom of the furnace, where it could cool and harden into a solid mass. From these ingots the metalsmiths cast and forged tools and weapons and ornaments. For the first time in Scotland the woodman's axe had a blade of bronze.

At first the metalsmiths worked with open moulds. Simple shapes were scooped out in blocks of soft stone. Into these they poured molten bronze and allowed it to cool. When it was set hard they knocked the castings from their moulds. Any roughness was trimmed off before polishing and sharpening. By this method they produced flat blades for knives and daggers which they riveted to handles of bone or horn or wood. Their axe heads too were cast flat and mounted in wooden shafts.

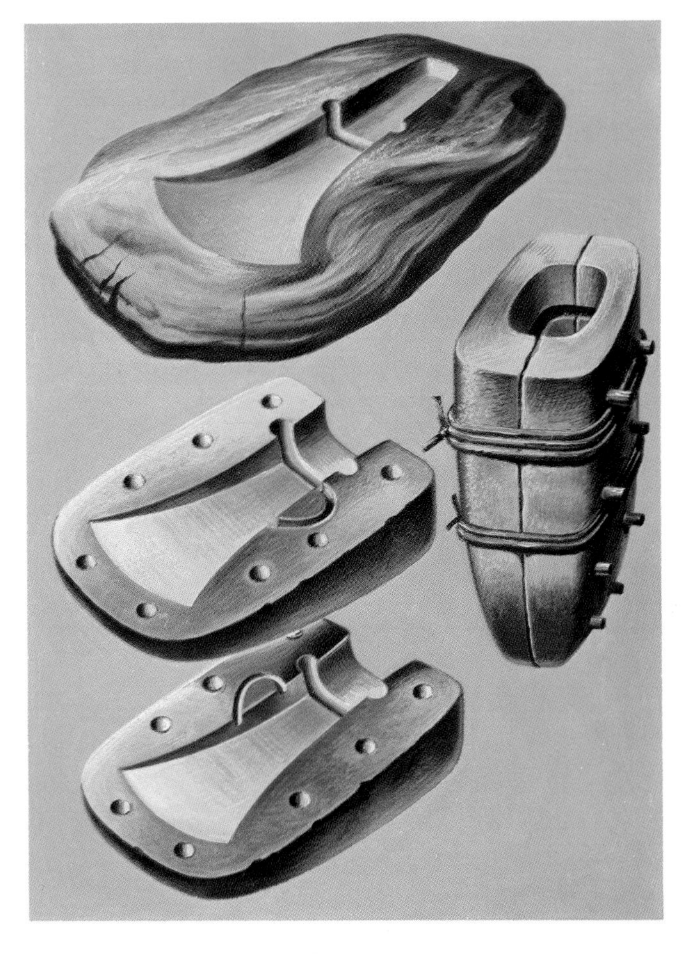

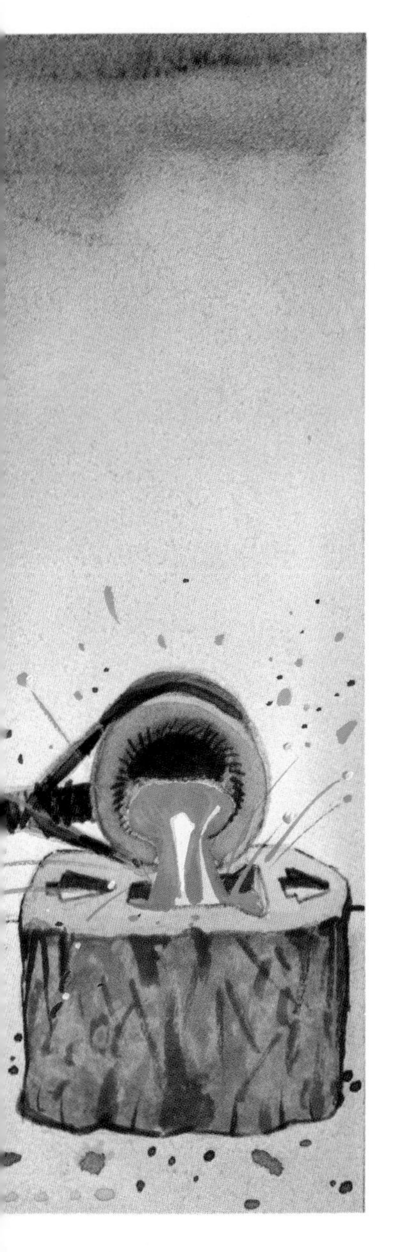

The smiths improved their craft. They invented new techniques and better designs. They added slender stabbing swords of bronze to the daggers, knives and spears with which they were already armed. They made carpenter's tools – chisels and gouges for cutting and bits for boring holes. Later still they produced a heavy slashing sword. The moulds they used now were in two halves which could be separated to release the castings and with these the metalsmiths produced an axe head with a socket into which the shaft could be firmly fixed. From thin sheets of beaten bronze they made ceremonial shields, helmets, kitchen utensils, cups, buckets, and cauldrons. They also made ornaments and fine jewellery from bronze and from gold: ear-rings and rings for the fingers and toes, necklaces, and decorated mounts for dagger hilts.

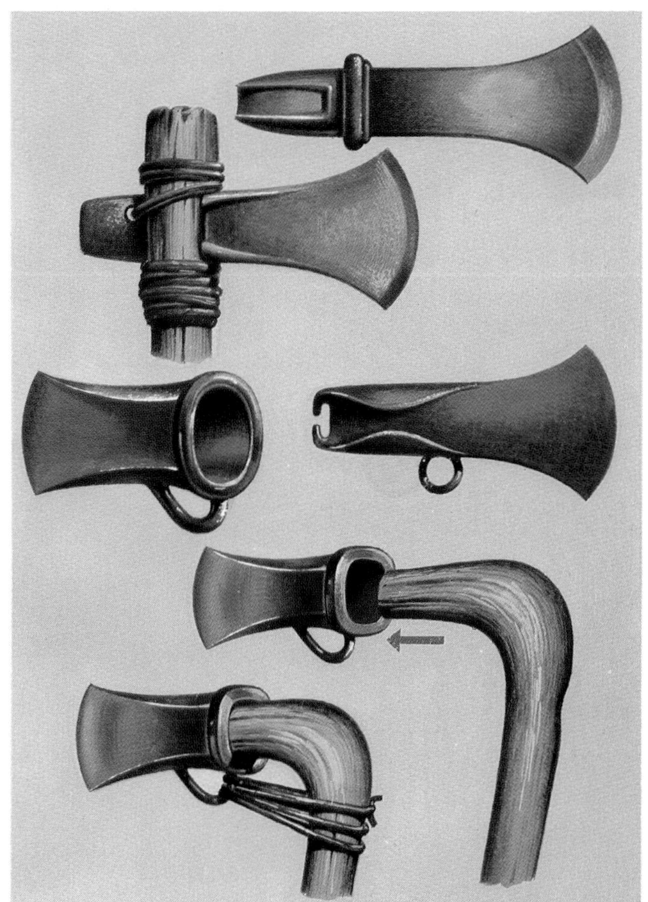

A new age

The fact that this new age had begun did not mean that the old one immediately ended. For some time Bronze Age and Stone Age methods worked side by side. In the windswept northerly Isles of Orkney the people of Skara Brae were quite unaffected by changes further south. On the mainland the Stone Age farmers living in the west and in the north still felled trees with flint axes and still raised great tombs of stone to honour their dead. And where they met the newcomers, there would be discussion and dispute, co-operation and conflict. Many centuries would pass before the better ways of the Bronze Age spread over all the land. But right from the beginning something did change, something which would influence our lifestyle from that time forward.

Bronze bucket from Flanders Moss in Perthshire

The idea of trade

The real difference between the Age of Bronze and all that had gone before was not simply that people had the use of better tools and weapons. The big change that now took place happened because people found that they had a problem. It was the way they solved it that changed our lives. The problem was this. Good stone for axe heads could be found in a great many places but the ores from which certain metals could be extracted were scarce and widely spread. Outcrops of copper and gold were not too far away. But to make bronze the metalsmiths required tin to mix with the copper and there was no tin anywhere in Scotland. The only place in the whole of Britain from which tin could be obtained was the most distant south-westerly tip, the part we now call Cornwall. Or supplies could be brought from the old homelands of the Bronze people across the North Sea. Either source was hundreds of miles away. Only by making special arrangements for importing tin could the metalsmiths ensure regular supplies. No one knows exactly how it was done; where the trade routes ran; how the merchants operated, or how many people were involved along the way. We do not even know if the tin was Cornish or Continental, but one thing is certain, for the first time in Scotland there lived a people who depended on trade.

Craftsmen

Within their little settlements in Scotland and throughout Europe a new kind of person now existed – the craftsman. Here was someone to be respected and to bring prestige to the whole tribe. He was a specialist, whose work was so important that he could be freed from the usual chores of food production to practise his skills for the benefit of the whole tribe.

And so the people who brought the Bronze Age to Scotland gave us not only a metal technology with which to improve our tools and ornaments, they also introduced international trade and our first specialist craftsmen.

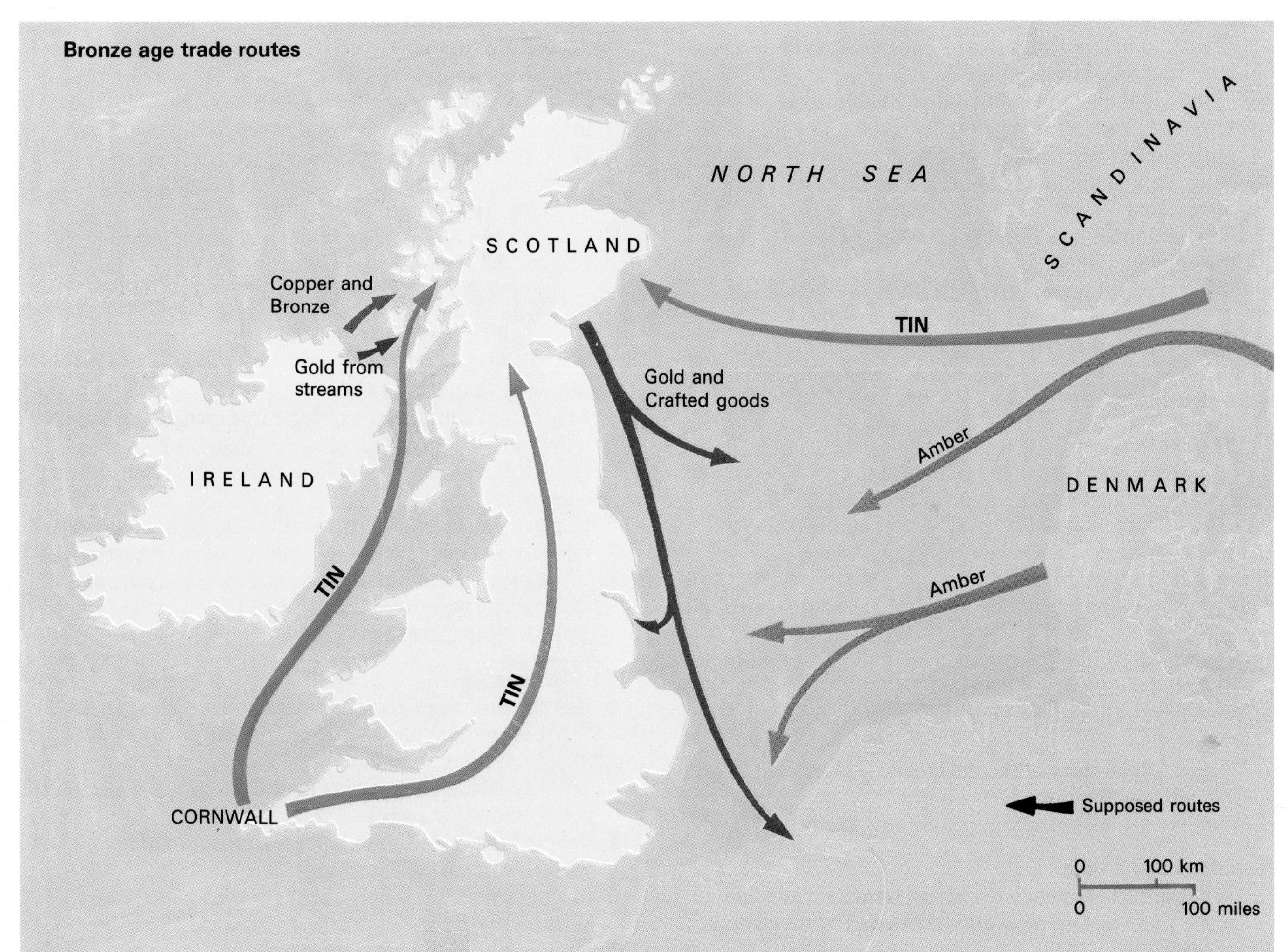

Workersection

The Long Thaw

Understand Your Work

The Hunters and the Ice Age

1 Why do you think that no one lived in Scotland fifteen thousand years ago?
2 In southern Europe, where people did live, how did they find food and shelter?
3 What happened that made it possible for people to live in ancient Scotland?
4 When people first came to Scotland the landscape they found was different from today's Scottish countryside. How?
5 Were the kinds of animals different too?
6 How do we know that some of the earliest people spent some time in what is now Fife?
7 How did these first settlers find their food and shelter? What did they eat?
8 Why did they move about so much?
9 Look at the maps on page 4. How did the landscape change in five thousand years?
10 Look at the finds from Morton Farm. Can you say how they were used?

Our First Farmers

1 What changes in the plains of Europe caused hunters to lose their usual food supply?
2 What did they do then instead of just hunting?
3 How did this alter their lifestyle?
4 How did the first farmers come to Scotland?
5 What special tool did they bring and why was it so important?
6 Why did these new farmers find their boats so useful for travel in Scotland?
7 What types of place did they settle in?
8 What crops and livestock did they raise?
9 Describe what is happening in the picture on page 8.
10 What is the difference between ancient and modern wheat and barley?

Skara Brae

1 Find Skara Brae on a map. When did the settlers first sail north to the Orkneys?
2 What were their usual types of shelter and why do you think they designed a new kind?
3 How did they build their new style of house?
4 How did it happen that we discovered the houses of Skara Brae?
5 What makes Skara Brae so important to people studying the early farmers of Scotland?
6 Why do you think they built their houses and furniture from stone?
7 What does the story of the modern housekeeper at Skara Brae tell you about the little houses?
8 What does it tell you about people now and people then?

Troubles and Trade

1 What things happened to ancient farmers that could make them feel helpless and threatened by mysterious powers?
2 How might they try to protect themselves against these 'great spirits'?
3 What did they construct at Maeshowe?
4 What does the work at Maeshowe tell you about how these farmers were organised?
5 Apart from hacking out a living space in the forest, what else did the stone axes cause to happen?
6 Why was an axe factory set up at Killin in Perthshire?
7 Where were the finished blades sent and for what might they have been exchanged?
8 What, in addition to stone axes, did the first farmers bring to Scotland?
9 Pretend you are the woman in the picture on page 12 and say how your house works.
10 Describe the tomb at Maeshowe.

Men of Bronze

The Newcomers

1 Why is the Stone Age given this name?
2 People who arrived in Scotland about 2000 BC brought new weapons and tools. What was special about them?
3 How did these newcomers reach Scotland?
4 Where did they enter and where did they settle?
5 How did they live in their settlements?
6 How were their special fires made and what were they for?
7 What new tool then appeared in Scotland?
8 What name was given to the new age that had begun in Scotland with the arrival of these newcomers?
9 Imagine you are the man in the picture on page 14. Explain what you are doing.

The Metalsmiths

1 What was the first type of mould used to cast bronze?
2 What work had still to be done to the axe blade when it came out of the mould?
3 Apart from axe heads, what else was made from bronze?
4 How were blades attached to their handles?
5 How did the later improved moulds differ from the first ones?
6 In what way did the new moulds make better axe heads?
7 Did the metalsmiths always shape bronze by casting it?
8 What other metal did they use and for what purpose?
9 Look at the pictures on page 15 and say how you would make a bronze axe.

The Bronze Age

1 Did the bronze axes replace the stone axe all at once?
2 What ingredient of bronze was difficult to find?
3 Where could it be found?
4 What special arrangements had to be made because this metal was so far away?
5 People in Scotland now depended on something new for their livelihood. What was it?
6 In the settlements a new kind of person had appeared. Who was he?
7 How was he able to find time to do his work?

8 Apart from metal tools, weapons and ornaments, what else did these men of bronze bring to mankind?
9 Look at the map on page 17 and say which goods were imported into bronze age Scotland, and from where.

Use Your Imagination

1 Ethra was a boy hunter who lived somewhere in the tundra plains of Europe. He liked to show off his skill by being the first to find good caves for shelter. When the story begins, he has just spotted a possible place . . .

Ethra felt excited; it was a ready-made shelter. And he had found it. He ran forward, slithering down the last few feet and ducked inside the cave. The air was cool and the light was dim. A good cave, he was sure, big and it smelt dry.

Suddenly, with a shock of fear, he was aware of another smell – a sour acrid smell. A cat smell!

He froze, tense with fear. Deep in the darkness something stirred. Ethra edged back towards the entrance, inch by inch.

His body moved into the light from outside. As it did so, there was a ferocious snarl and a rush.

He glimpsed two yellow eyes as he turned to run . . .

What happened next? Did Ethra escape or not, with or without help? What did his parents say? What warnings were given to others? Think about these things and finish off the story.

2 Animals are usually swifter or stronger or fiercer than people and they have sharper hearing and a better sense of smell. How do you think hunters were able to catch and kill them? How did they find them, get close enough and what weapons would they need?

3 The Stone Age Hunters could not write but they could draw and their pictures would say something. See if you can draw some simple pictures to pass on information or give instructions. You could show how to make an axe or what dangers to look out for when exploring a cave or . . .

4 The hunters brought back the beasts they had killed, for food. What other uses might the people find for parts of animals that could not be eaten – hide, bones etc?

5 People sometimes make up stories explaining things they do not properly understand. These stories are called legends. Write your own legend explaining how the hunters first got 'fire' or 'animals to hunt' or the 'axe' or . . .
Perhaps they were gifts from the gods and spirits or stolen by a mighty hunter of old or . . .

6 Unfinished meals and valuable tools and ornaments found in Skara Brae suggest that the people left the little township in a great hurry. What do you imagine could have happened to cause this?

7 Why do you think the Stone Age craftsmen made axe blades of polished jadeite which were beautiful but useless? Do we make things like this today?

8 Can you think of how people may have discovered that metal could be melted out of certain stones?
Could you write a story about this?

Further Work

1 Some hunters painted animals on their cave walls and showed themselves to be artists of the highest quality. You can try being a cave painter too. Crumple up a large piece of paper to make it rough and uneven like a cave wall. Of course, you will have to make your own paints and brushes from things *hunters* could find. Then choose an animal, one you think you would like to paint for its beauty or its strength. Make your own painting.

2 Hunters carry or look for material to build shelters from. You can design the best shelter for hunters. You will need a shallow box with sand and a group of large stones so that you can experiment. The stones are rocks and the sand is the ground.

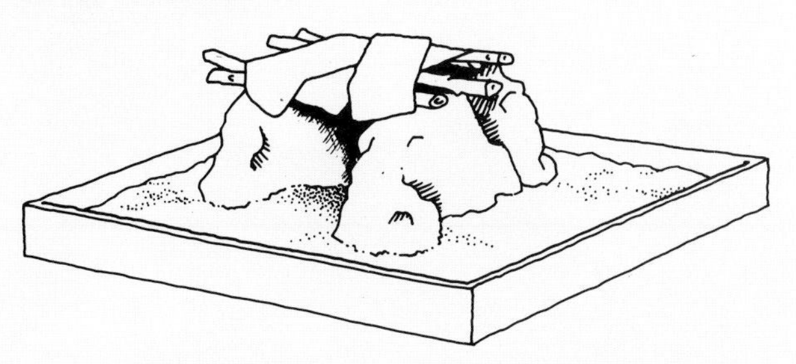

You'll need also the kind of things the hunters would have – *twigs* (for poles or little trees), paper (for skins). See how many types of shelter your group can make models of.

3 Write a poem about a night spent in your shelter on your first hunt. First imagine you are huddled in the shelter and think about this . . .
Now begin the poem with a line that says where you are.
Then go on to describe . . .

> The weather – cold and stormy or hot and still, or . . .
> Say what you hear, smell, see
> Say what you imagine you see or hear
> Say what you are thinking.

You could finish with something unexpected happening and the poem might be called 'The First Night', 'The First Hunt' . . . or whatever you think of.

4 Bronze Age people made very attractive pottery. They did not have a potter's wheel and you can use their method to make your own pots. All you need is plasticine and a pencil.
Roll some plasticine into a long 'snake' and then coil it up for the base –

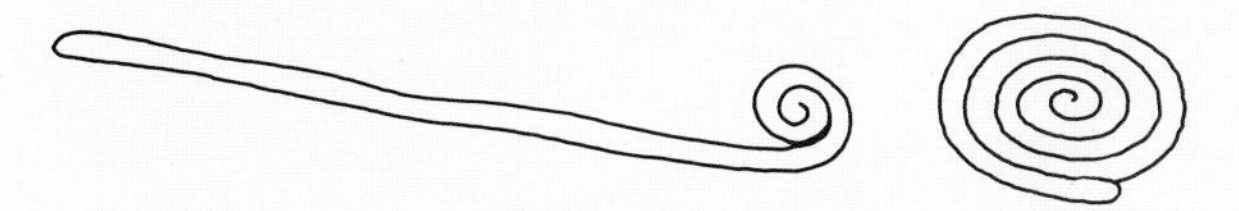

Then coil more plasticine to make the pot. Use the pencil to make patterns which join the coils together.

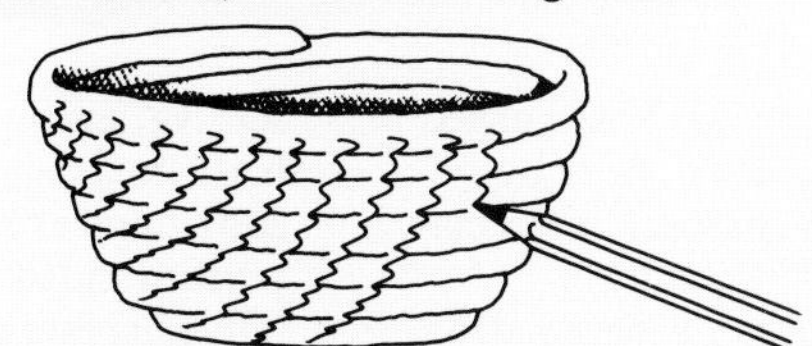

Make a display of your group's pots.

The Iron Warlords

The iron ore was first crushed and then packed, layer by layer with charcoal, into a clay furnace. With goatskin bellows the fire was blasted to a heat intense enough to melt off the slag, leaving the metal like a blackened sponge. With heat and hammer blows this was purified and forged into implements of iron – a metal not only harder than bronze but plentiful and cheap. The smelting furnace was about ½ m in diameter scooped out in the floor to a depth of twenty or so cms. A pair of goatskin bellows blasted air in to the fire through two pipes with clay nozzles. Here the iron was separated from the ore, later to be reheated in another fire and hammered to shape on the anvil.

The Bronze Age in Scotland continued for more than a thousand years. People lived out their days in simple communities scattered throughout their darkly forested land. Little changed. The same type of houses were built for shelter. The same chores were performed for survival. Only in the craft and trade of metalwork was there any real advance. By 800 BC in foundries and forges throughout the land new methods were being used to manufacture better tools and weapons, finer ornaments and utensils. Trade in axe heads and tin thrived between the communities and with the people of other lands across the sea.

Iron

But something else was happening in 800 BC. Far to the east in that part of the continent now called Austria lived a warrior people who were to dominate Europe for almost a thousand years. These people had learned how to mine a special ore from which a hard black metal could be extracted – iron. Armed with their new iron weapons these fierce and hostile tribes were to raid and plunder Europe for centuries to come. They fought their way from the shores of the Black Sea in the east, to Ireland 2,000 miles away in the west. The Celtic warlords had arrived and with them Europe entered the Age of Iron.

The forge

And now in Scotland, for the first time, there was a new kind of workshop in which tools and weapons of iron were made – the blacksmith's forge. The working of iron was a craft very different from that of copper or bronze. Iron would not melt in any furnace known to the smiths and so could not be poured into moulds and cast. Nor was it possible to shape or bend the cold iron as had been done with copper. A new way of handling and working the material was needed. Shapes previously cast had now to be wrought by hammer. Just to handle the glowing metal required the invention of tongs. But the blacksmiths were truly the masters of iron. They cut and formed it to their design. They controlled its very nature, for they could make the metal hard and brittle or soft and pliable by judging exactly how long to hold it in the high heat of the charcoal forge. What is more, they learned to combine the two types, layer upon layer, like plywood so that a hard yet pliable metal was forged; a metal fit to take a keen edge for tool or weapon; a metal with which to make rims for chariot wheels; a metal called steel. The ring of the blacksmith's hammer now joined with the sound of the woodman's axe throughout the land.

The Celts

The warrior tribes came to Scotland and they settled. Wave upon wave of them surged over the land during the centuries before Christ. Some, who came as early as 700 BC, landed on the Scottish coast around the Moray Firth. Others struck north from England, probably by sea, to enter at the mouth of the River Tweed. From these earliest days to the first century BC the whole of south Scotland, right to where the Highlands begin, was gradually covered in a rash of small settlements cut from the woodland with axes of iron.

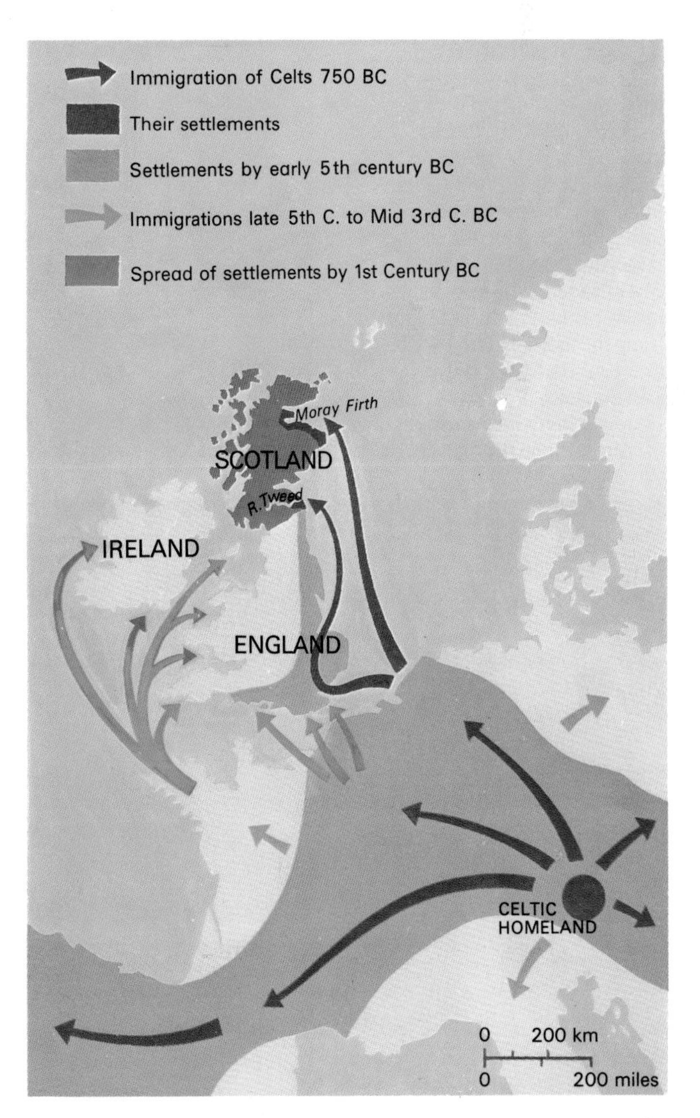

Houses

The houses they lived in were round, some only six or so paces across and others as much as fifteen. The thatched roof was supported on a ring of strong upright timbers set firmly around a tall centre post. In larger houses more than one ring of supports was used to bear the greater weight of the roof. Walls were made from a kind of basket-weave panel called a wattle hurdle over which soft clay was daubed to seal out the weather. Some houses may have been walled in timber. The floor was hard dry clay and towards the centre where the roof was highest a small fire burned in the stone hearth. The smoke may have passed through a hole in the roof shielded somehow from the Scottish rain, or perhaps escaped through openings on either side. It may even have been that only the door provided ventilation. Above the fire on a chain of wrought iron hung a bronze cauldron in which joints of salted pork could be boiled. To the side on a wooden table lay the heavy stone mill wheel called a quern under which corn was ground into flour. Close by, on another table, dough for bread-making was kneaded, later to be baked in clay ovens. Against the walls hung the tools for daily work – sickles and scythes, knives, axes and hoes. For seating and sleeping there were warm rugs of animal fur on the dry clay floor.

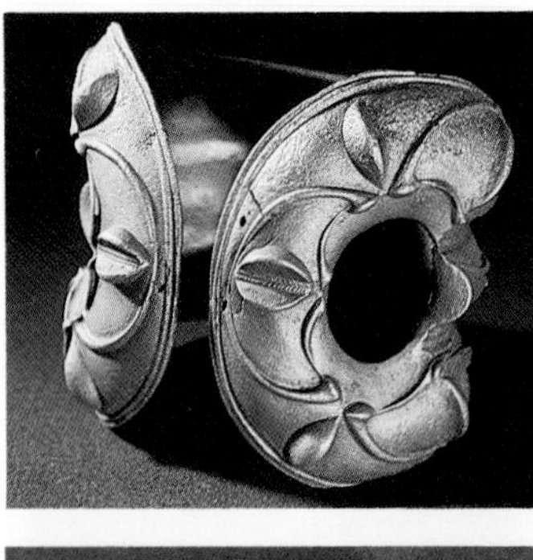

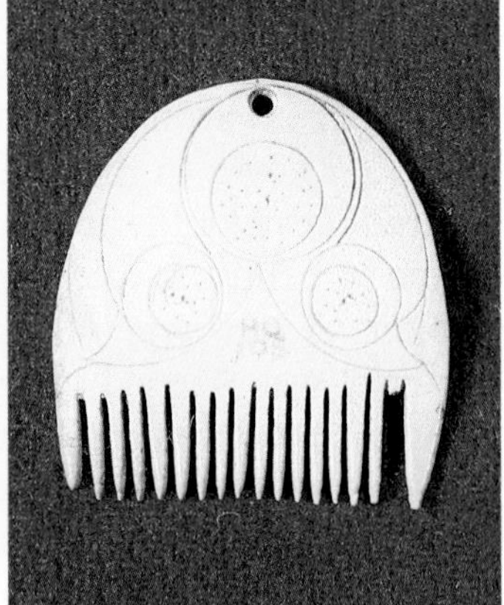

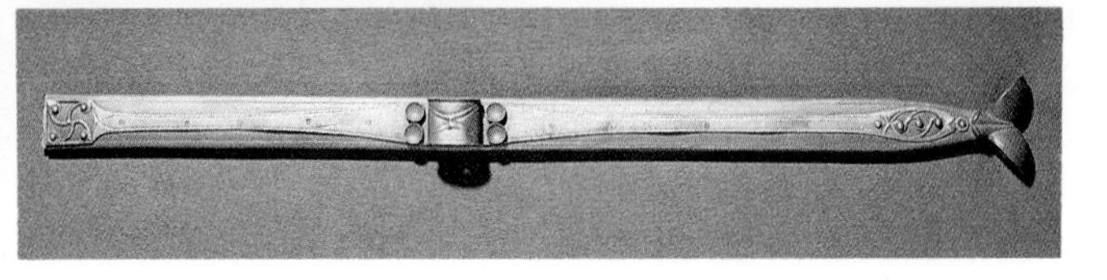

The Celts still worked in bronze and gold too. They made the finest utensils and weapons, ornaments and jewellery, decorated with strange and beautiful patterns.

Early settlements

In each settlement there were usually a dozen or so houses surrounded by a stout timber palisade to keep out warlike neighbours. To the north and west also, and in the islands beyond, where there were few trees, the building was of stone, though to much the same design. Celtic settlers lived very much like the Bronze Age farmers, tilling the soil with simple hoes to raise crops of wheat, oats and barley. In Scotland they did not use the plough for many centuries. They tended herds and flocks of cattle, sheep, goats and pigs, and depended for food on this livestock much more than on their scanty crops.

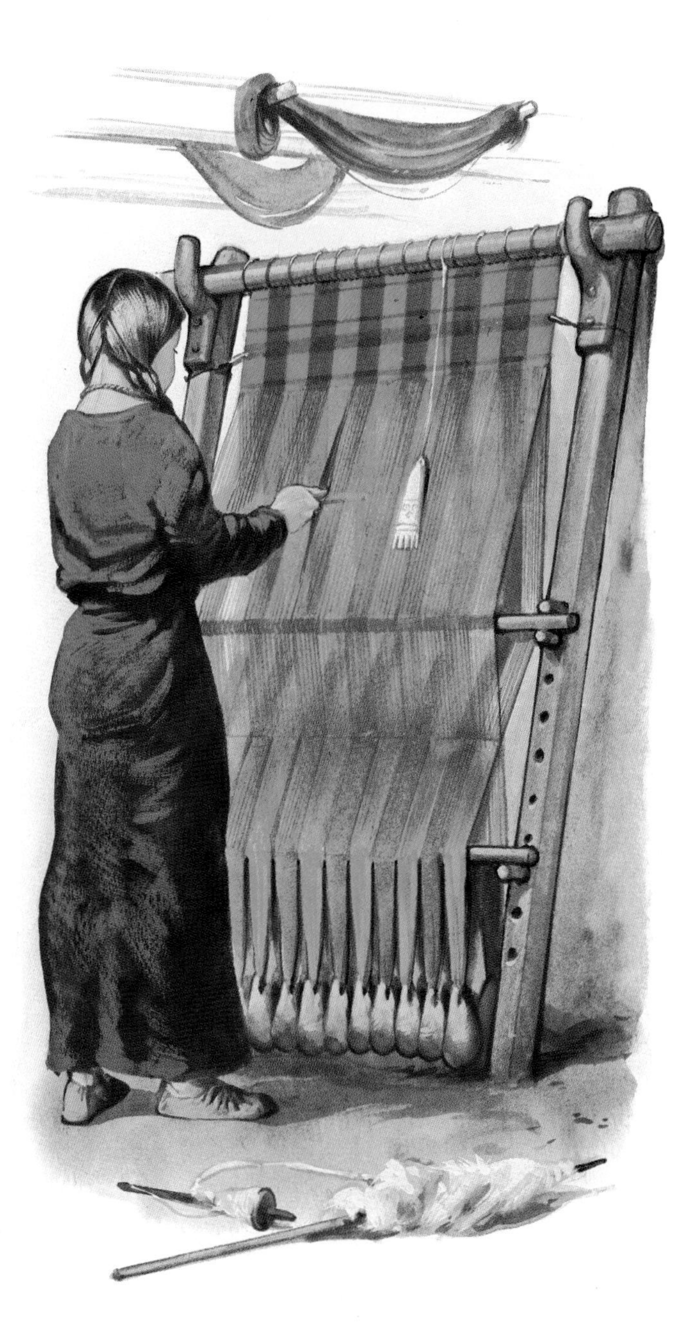

Weaving and leatherwork

In each house stood a strong wooden frame. From its topmost cross bar hung threads, each pulled taut by a weight of stone or baked clay hanging near the floor. On this, fleece, shorn from the sheep with an iron knife and spun into yarn, was woven to make woollen fabric. With a wooden shuttle the weft thread of the richly coloured yarn was lead to and fro under one and over the next of the weighted warp threads, which were raised and lowered to let the shuttle pass easily. On such looms were made the bright garments worn by the Iron Age Celts. They wove other materials too, though not on looms – basketwork and matting from rushes; wattle hurdles to be used for walling from thin or split branches. And they worked in leather, making clothes and harness and also containers which were easier to carry than those of pottery – important to a people often on the move.

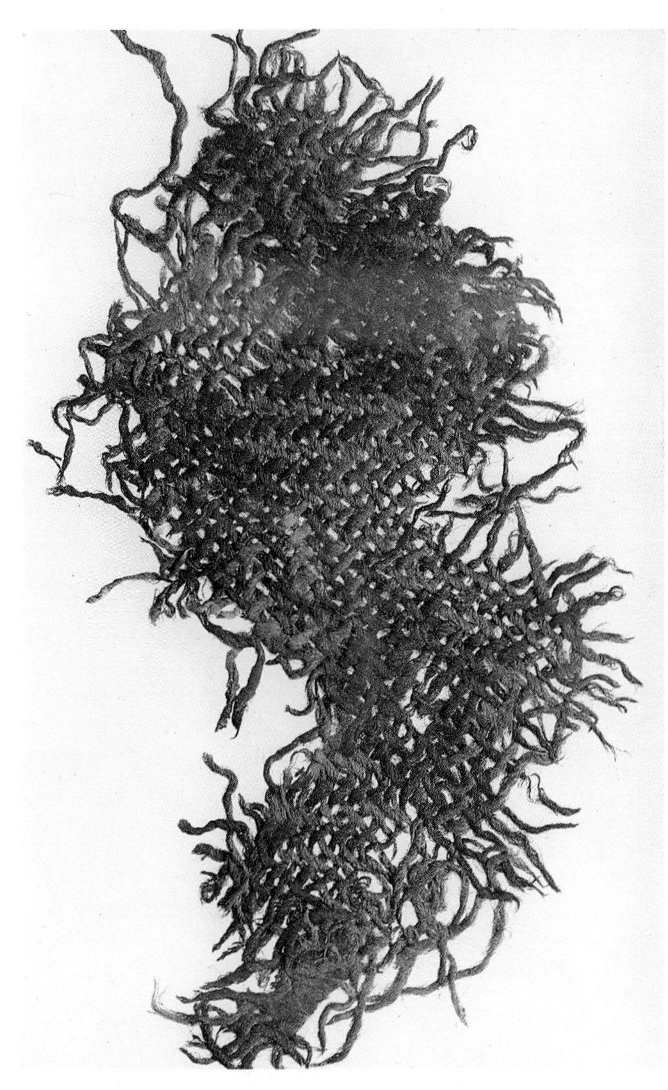

Hillforts

The Celts brought a new feature to Scotland's landscape. On high ground now appeared the Celtic hillforts. Over the centuries to come more than fifteen hundred would be built, some smaller than a football pitch and others twenty or more times that area enclosing whole villages or towns. The Celts were a warlike people given to tribal quarrels and cattle raiding. They thought it wise to prepare their defences well.

right: Eildon Hill today

In the forest woodcutters laboured long hours, swinging their heavy iron axes. The felled trees were shorn of their branches and dragged away by teams of straining oxen. In quarries stone was cut and split with iron chisels and hammers to be carted away, load after load. Up the hillsides these supply trains laboured, towards the summit where carpenters were at work erecting a massive framework of the felled timber which laced together a growing wall of rubble, more than three metres high and five thick. Masons faced the wall with fitted blocks of solid stone as it gradually enclosed the hill top in its sweep. For the entrance to this great circle of stone the carpenters constructed thick wooden gates, taller than the walls, behind which people and herds might safely shelter from attack by the spearmen of neighbouring tribes.

above: Dun Telve broch in Inverness-shire

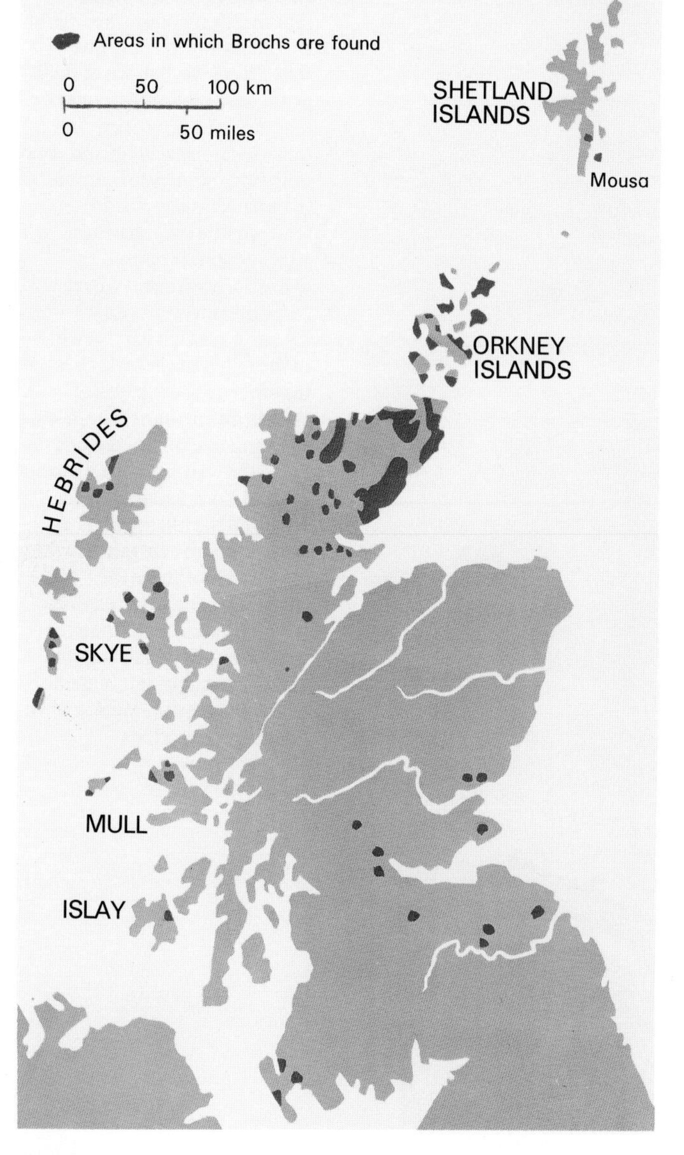

Brochs

On a small still island east of the Shetlands, a massive stone tower broods heavily over the craggy shore just as it did more than two thousand years ago. This lonely monument is the Broch of Mousa. Because it is there we know that people once occupied that bleak and lonely island, Celtic people of our Iron Age. We know also that they greatly feared some enemy. Beyond this we may only guess. And not only in Mousa but in Caithness, Shetland, Orkney and the Western Isles more than 500 of these great fortresses, silently proclaim a secret history. All brochs are built to the same general design, like the one in this picture. Always they stand on good fertile farmland. Seldom are they far from the edge of the sea. Nowhere in the world save Scotland are such structures to be found.

A detective story

For many years archaeologists and historians have tried to solve the mystery of the brochs and of the enemy against whom they were constructed. Like good detectives they have searched for clues.

Clearly brochs were intended for defence. But defence against whom – or what? As the detective would ask – Who had the means, the opportunity and the motive to attack?

These huge towering walls may be fifteen or more metres high. Surely they were meant to keep out more than a spear! The low, narrow entrance tunnel would prevent the use of a battering ram. No team of men could work in such a small space. And if there was no way through door or walls, perhaps over the top? Again this had been thought of. Scaling ladders, perhaps eighteen metres long, would be too difficult to handle. Whoever built the brochs guarded against an enemy who could use such and other engines of war.

The brochs are seldom far from the shore. Did then the feared attackers come by sea? Now the detective's identikit picture shows two features – engines of war and the use of ships.

And then there is the inner courtyard about eight metres wide. Not large enough certainly to hold livestock and store grain. What then was the prize that this unknown attacker was seeking? What was his motive? Perhaps it was the people themselves; people to be turned into slaves for some great empire.

Now the identikit image is clear. The suspect has a description – an organized enemy with engines of war and sea-going transport who is seeking slaves. There was certainly a people who fitted that description; a people with the most feared and best organized armies in the world and with an expanding empire in need of slaves – the Romans.

But could the Romans have been in the right place at the right time? Had they the opportunity?

Two thousand years ago the Romans were invading and subduing Britain and a Roman historian called Tacitus wrote at the time that slaves were one of the prizes of the Roman Conquest of Britain. He also mentioned the Orcades which is another name for Orkney. The Romans had the opportunity, the means and the motive. They must therefore be under suspicion. The case remains to be proved and the investigations still continue, but certainly the broch would be an effective defence against such attacks.

But this is not the only mystery surrounding the brochs. For example no one is certain exactly who were the broch builders. We know they were there and we have seen what they could do because they left their mark, but that is about as far as we may go.

One other mystery and perhaps the most exciting is in the simple statement – there were more than five hundred of these mighty fortresses all built to a standard design. Where did the standard design come from? Did it form in the mind of one master mason as an idea and then a plan which would provide perfect security using only the rough hewn slabs scattered on a treeless landscape. Are we perhaps straining to dimly see, across two thousand years, one unnamed man to whom more than five hundred monuments were raised. And even if we could identify this stone builder, would we then know how so many brochs were built by so few people in such a limited time?

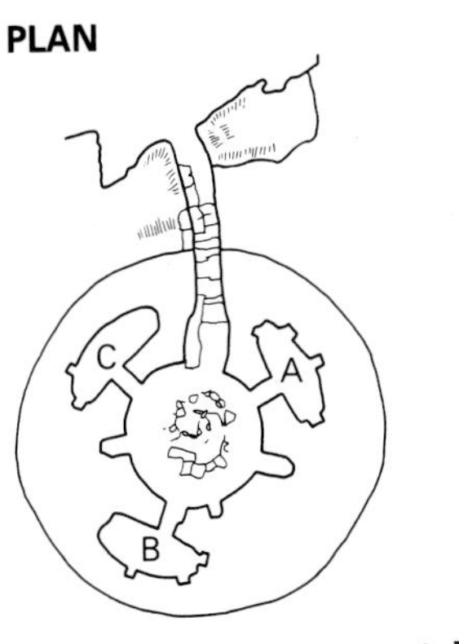

below far left: Broch of Mousa today.
The illustration shows part of a cross-section of a reconstruction of the Broch of Mousa. Here and in the plan (**below left** A, B & C) you can see hollows built in the thick walls to house the defenders.

Crannogs

The Celts had other, perhaps even better, ways to make safe their living place. In Kirkcudbright, in the south-west of Scotland, there is a stretch of water called Milton Loch. Here, as in other places, another form of defence was constructed. A great raft of logs and brushwood was floated on the marshy surface of the water. Round it a fence of timber posts was driven into the bed of the loch. On this island of wood a thatched house was built fifteen metres in diameter. Round its timber walls there was a walkway and on the far side, a harbour. The shore was reached by a narrow causeway. The people who lived there tilled the nearby fields but could withdraw to the safety of their man-made island, called a crannog, should danger threaten.

Remains of the crannog at Milton Loch, photographed in 1953

The tribes

From the fastness of their crannogs, hilltop towns and forts, the Celts came forth in conflict. They were always ready to settle in battle old scores and new, or raid and plunder the herds and flocks of neighbouring tribes. The Celts dominated most of Europe for hundreds of years, but not as an empire. They were never one nation with one leader. From the very beginning they were a people of independent spirit who, as their numbers grew, formed clans from families and nearby tribes. Each tribe was a kingdom in itself sharing a language with all the others but offering little friendship.

Scotland now had at least sixteen such tribes. They were loyal to their own kings and queens and possessed their own gathering places where men could meet to exchange goods and produce and to hear the latest news! In the lowlands of south Scotland there were four tribes. The Damnonii lived in

the west, in an area covering from what is now Ayrshire to the Clyde. Further south were the Novantae, who ruled all Galloway and Dumfries. On the other side of the country along the east coast stretched the lands of the Votadini, as far to the north as the River Forth, with their tribal capital on a hill in East Lothian called Traprain Law. Twenty or so miles west of this was another Votadinian centre at Din Eidyn. We call it Edinburgh. About thirty miles due south of Traprain Law on the north face of Eildon Hill overlooking the River Tweed, stood another of these great tribal centres but this time it belonged to the fourth of the southern tribes – the Selgovae. They held the hill country between the Votadini in the east and the two west coast tribes.

Scotland, beyond the Forth and the Clyde, was the homeland for a further twelve tribes, from the Epidii in the Mull of Kintyre to the Cornovii away to the north-east in Caithness; from the Cerones of the Western Highlands to the Taezali whose territory we now call Aberdeenshire. Not a nation, but a land harbouring sixteen kingdoms usually at war with one another. Throughout this time, Scotland shook with the noise of battle – the harsh blare of carnyx, (the Celtic war trumpet) and the hard thunder of hooves and chariot wheels.

During these seven centuries the Celtic tribes of this land, made their mark so deeply that it would never be erased. At once artist and warrior; cattle-thief and craftsman; hunter and poet, the fierce and fearless Celt was most of all a human being of independent soul, unwilling to yield to the pomp and majesty of some great king or to the laws and taxes of a distant government, giving loyalty only to kinfolk and tribe. While the peoples who had populated Scotland before had brought many new ideas, the Celts, more than any, laid the foundation on which would be built the Scottish nationality. Even to-day Celtic blood flows abundantly in the veins of the Scottish people.

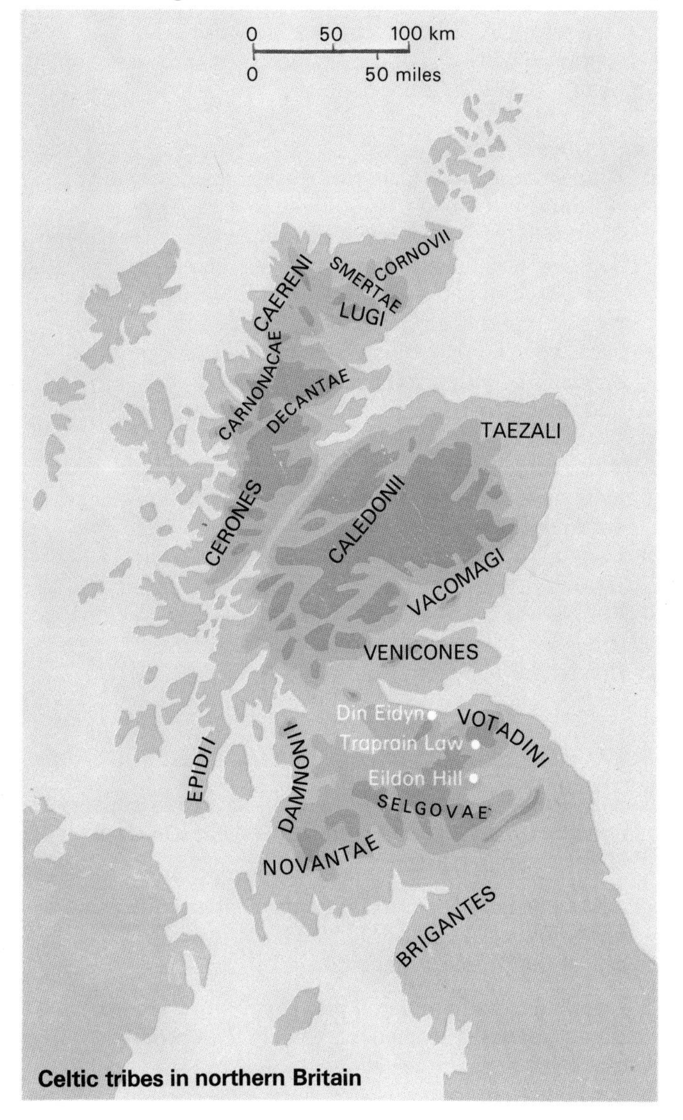

Celtic tribes in northern Britain

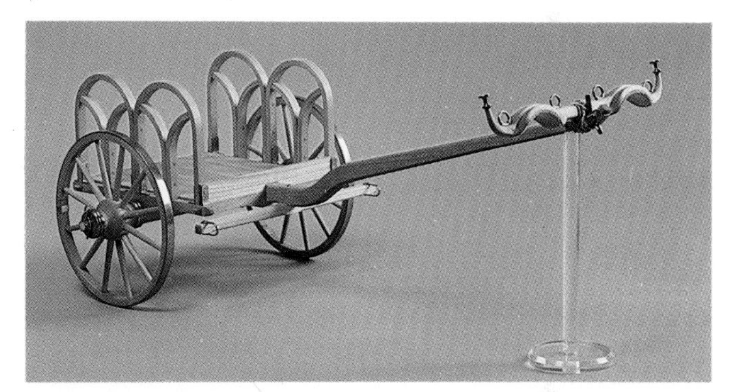

above: Reconstruction of Celtic chariot
below: Bronze horse bit from Burnswark in Dumfries
right: Remains of a carnyx from Deskford in Banff. It has been partly reconstructed.

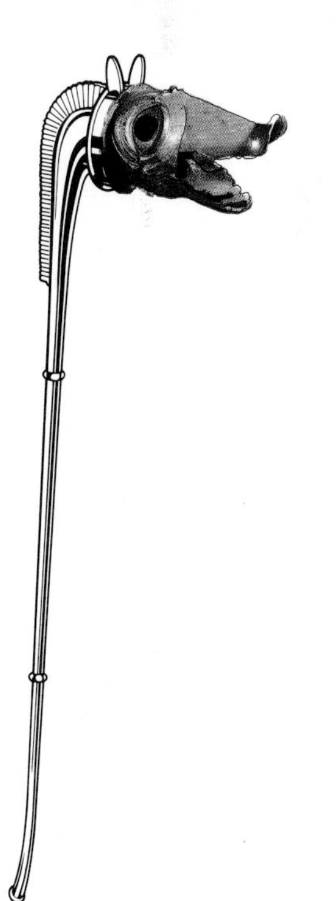

Worksection

The Iron Warlords

Understand Your Work

Another Age

1 For how long did the Bronze Age last in Scotland?
2 There was little progress during this period, in the way people lived and laboured, except in one type of work. Which?
3 Did trade do well in the Bronze Age?
4 Who were the people who came westwards across Europe to Scotland about 700 BC?
5 What new age started with them?
6 What special skill and knowledge did they bring with them?
7 In what two ways was their new metal better than bronze?
8 Were the newcomers farmers, too?
9 Imagine you are the boy in the picture on page 20. Say what you and the others are doing.
10 Look at the map on page 21. Which were the earliest parts of Scotland to be settled by the Celts?

The Newcomers

1 Where did the newcomers enter Scotland?
2 How big were the settlements they usually built in Scotland?
3 What crops did they raise?
4 What livestock did they keep?
5 How did they turn the soil for planting crops in Scotland?
6 For what purpose did the Celts raise horses?
7 What was the usual way of protecting the little villages?
8 From whom did they have to be protected?
9 Look at the pictures on page 23. Can you explain how the loom works?

Celtic Homes

1 With what did the Celts build their houses?
2 What shape were their houses?
3 Why would the fire be low-burning and not blazing cheerfully?
4 What were the cooking and baking arrangements in the little dwellings?
5 What other crafts were practised in the home?
6 Apart from cloth, what else did the Celts weave?
7 How did the houses in the north and in the Western Isles differ from the others? Why do you think this was so?
8 What is a quern?
9 Imagine you are one of the people in the picture on page 22. Describe your home and some of the objects we can see.

A New Craft

1 How did the Celtic metalsmiths make their special fires hot enough to extract iron?
2 Did the heat melt the iron?
3 What name is given to the way in which metal is shaped by heating and hammering?
4 Why did the Celts not shape iron by casting?
5 Was iron the only metal they used?
6 How did they make their furnaces?
7 What fuel did they use in their furnaces?
8 What caused the Celtic metalsmith to invent tongs?
9 Describe three of the objects on page 22. What do you think they were used for?

Defence

1 What was the new feature the Celts brought to the Scottish landscape?
2 What was it about the Celts that made it necessary to protect their villages?
3 Mightier hillforts use more than a wooden fence to keep attackers out. How were their walls constructed?
4 A very special kind of defence was built mainly in the north and all to the same design. What are they called?
5 Where is the best example of this kind of structure to be found?
6 What name is given to the special kind of defence used at Milton Loch?
7 How was this constructed?
8 What weapons did the Celtic warriors use?
9 Imagine you are one of the characters in the picture on page 24. Say what is happening.

The Tribes

1 Who were the four Celtic tribes who lived in south Scotland?
2 Make a list of the names of all sixteen tribes who live in Scotland and see how many you can memorise.
3 The Votadini had a great centre at Din Edyn. What do we now call this place?
4 See if you can find which tribe occupied the part of Scotland in which you live.
5 Did the Celtic tribes live at peace with one another?
6 What is a carnyx?
7 What vehicle did the Celtic warlords use in battle?
8 How were the wooden wheels protected from wear on the rough ground?
9 Look at the pictures of brochs on pages 26 and 27. Describe how they were defended.
10 Look at the map of Celtic tribes on page 29. Which tribes live in the Highlands? Which live in the Lowlands?

Use Your Imagination

1 The horses of ancient Britain were small and not very suitable for riding. How did the Celtic warlords manage to use them in battle?

2 The Celts held the secrets of iron working and iron was cheap and easily found. How did this help the Celts to defeat the Bronze Age people in battle?

3 Iron had to be hammered into shape while red hot. See if you can design some tools to help the Celtic blacksmith. Make a drawing of each and say what it is for.

4 Metal expands when it is heated and shrinks again when it cools. How would the Celtic blacksmith use this idea to make sure the iron rims round chariot wheels gripped really tightly?

5 The great stone walls of hillforts in Scotland were held together by a framework of massive wooden beams. How might this be a serious weakness? Write a note explaining how you could use this idea to attack a hillfort.
See if you can find out what a vitrified fort is.

6 When Celts stormed hillforts and failed to break through they usually gave up and went away. Can you imagine why the Celtic warrior peoples did not lay siege to the hillforts and wait patiently until the inmates surrendered?

7 How would you design the causeway that led from the shore to the crannog so that it would be difficult for attackers to use? Could you hide it in any way?

8 What tools do you think the Celts would need to quarry and cut stone for their hillforts? Make drawings of your ideas and write a caption explaining each.

9 Why were leather bags easier to carry than clay pots?

10 Make a list of the various kinds of work done by the men and women of a Celtic settlement.

Further Work

1 The early Celtic peoples did not read or write, yet they managed to pass down from one generation to the next all the details of their complicated laws and customs. How do you suppose they did this? (Think about how you came to know all those nursery rhymes.)
If you were an ancient Celt, what sort of plan could you make to be sure that none of these details were lost? Would it be left to everybody to attend to or would there be special people for this job? Write a note on your ideas.

2 Hillforts were surrounded by stout fences or even stone walls which gave strong protection from attack, but there was a weakness. There has to be a way in and out! Your group can now be hillfort designers and 'invent' your own systems for protecting the gate, just as the Celts did.
You will need a large tray and a mound of damp sand for your hill; lots of little drinking straws to use as posts for the fence round the hillfort. Now make a complete ring of posts for your fort and then remove some for the gate. The Celts used a kind of maze to protect the gate.

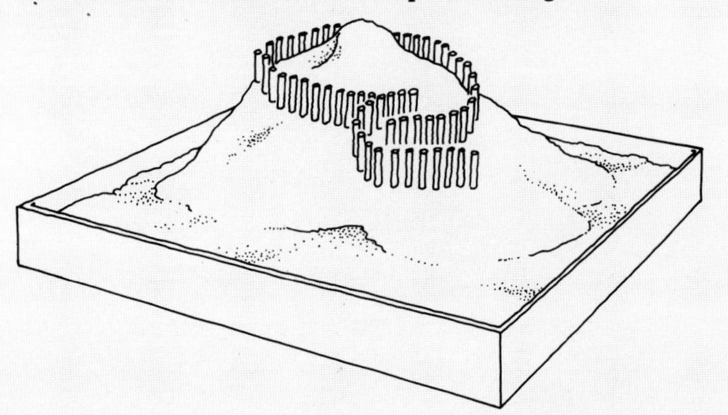

Work out your defensive maze and when you have agreed on the best design, make notes on how it would make attack more difficult and defence easier.

3 When the chief dies a new one must be ready to take over at once or there may be jealousy and fighting within the tribe making it an easy target for enemies. Imagine that your group are members of a Celtic tribe whose old chief has just died but no one has been chosen to succeed him, though there are plenty of people who wish to! This is a dangerous time for your tribe. Each group member now paints a portrait of one of these people and writes a little speech saying why he is the best choice. At the end of your speech this question should be answered –

> 'If you are chosen to be chief, how will you make sure that everyone knows and agrees who will be the next chief after you, and the next after that, and so on . . .?'

Make a display of your pictures and speeches and let your tribe (class) make the choice.

4 At night in the smoky warmth of their homes, the Celts would gather round the fire and tell stories of great deeds and terrible events. A hunter would describe how he slew a giant boar, or someone else talk of the evil thing that lurks in the black woods, or tell of secret places or enchanted pools or . . . You write your own story to thrill the people gathered round your fire.

5 Each year on the 1st January the Celts held a festival called Imbolg. And every three months they had another. Next was Beltane, on May Day, then Lugnasa in mid August, and Samhain, on the first day of November. In their year Samhain was the first and most important. They believed that on the evening before Samhain evil spirits were about and magic was strong, so the people performed strange rituals to protect themselves. What happens nowadays on that night? Do you think we still remember what our forefathers were up to!
Find out as much as you can about these festivals and how they have affected our modern Scotland.

The Romans

Claudius's invasion of Britain AD 43

The Iron Age Celts had been living out their lives and fighting their eternal fights in this bleak and rugged land for eight centuries while, far to the south-east across the sea, great events had been taking place which were soon to change the face of Britain. In AD 43, at a port called Boulogne on the north coast of Gaul, there was tremendous activity. The air was filled with the sound of soldiers marching and the quay-side bustle of ships loading. In the river mouth and in the harbour a great fleet rode at anchor. There were heavy transports and lighter warships with oars, which could be easily beached. Through the days and weeks the urgent preparation went on. Company upon company of troops arrived and the quay-side was piled high with supplies and equipment until at last the large army was assembled. The invaders were ready, a mighty force of the world's best fighting soldiers, the soldiers of the Legions of Rome. Altogether, more than forty thousand men were assembled to embark for the crossing when weather and tide were right.

The Legions

This was not the first Roman invasion fleet to approach the British shore. Twice before under Julius Caesar, the Legions struck at the south coast, though with no great success. The first time was in 55 BC in late August, the second a year later in 54 BC. But these two early invasions had no effect on the Celtic peoples of the north. It was to be the Legions now approaching the British coast that would in years to come strike north into the heart of Scotland.

Claudius

Julius Caesar

For the conquest of Britain the Emperor Claudius had ordered to Boulogne the Second legion, called the Augusta, from Strasburg on the river Rhine, the Fourteenth legion, the Gemina, from Mainz and the Twentieth, Valeria Victrix, from Cologne, and finally, from Pannonia on the Upper Danube, the Ninth, the Hispana.
Each legion had five thousand six hundred highly trained, well armed men, divided in companies of eighty, each under the command of a centurion. The foot soldiers wore a metal helmet and plate armour made of metal strips. They carried a rectangular shield, two spears, a short stabbing sword and a dagger. There was also a small unit of about one hundred and twenty cavalry.
In addition to the legions there were regiments of auxiliaries. They were not Roman citizens but were recruited throughout the Empire and fought with their native weapons but with the benefit of Roman training discipline and strategy.

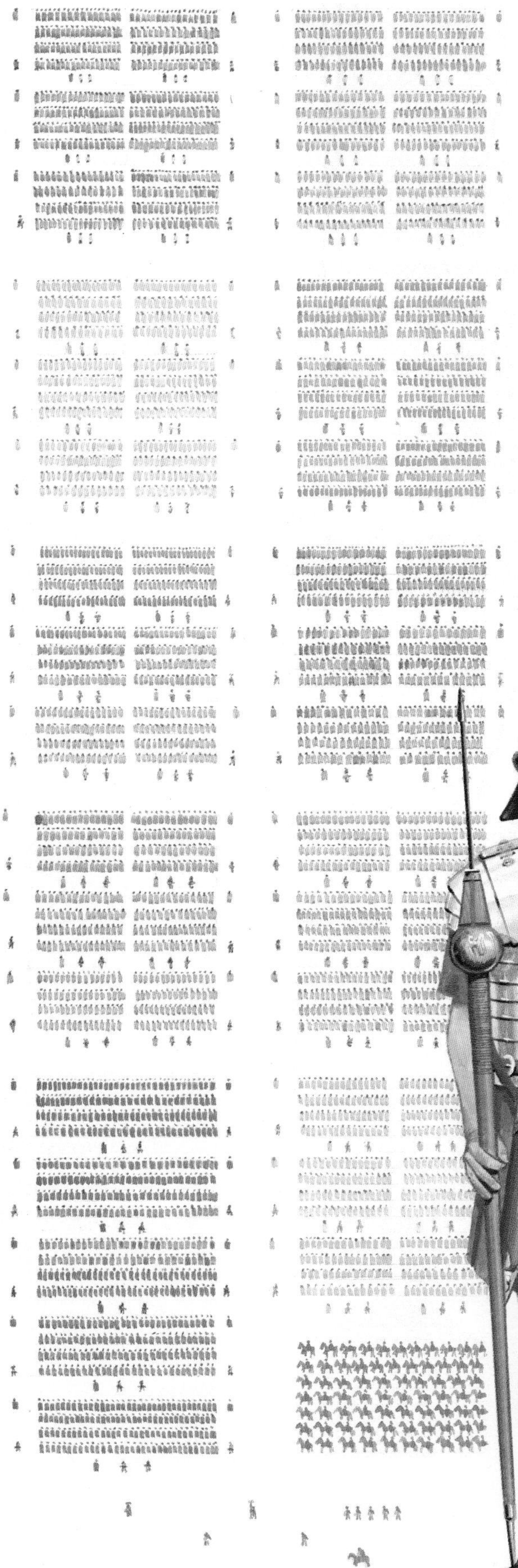

The composition of a legion

The conquest of southern Britain

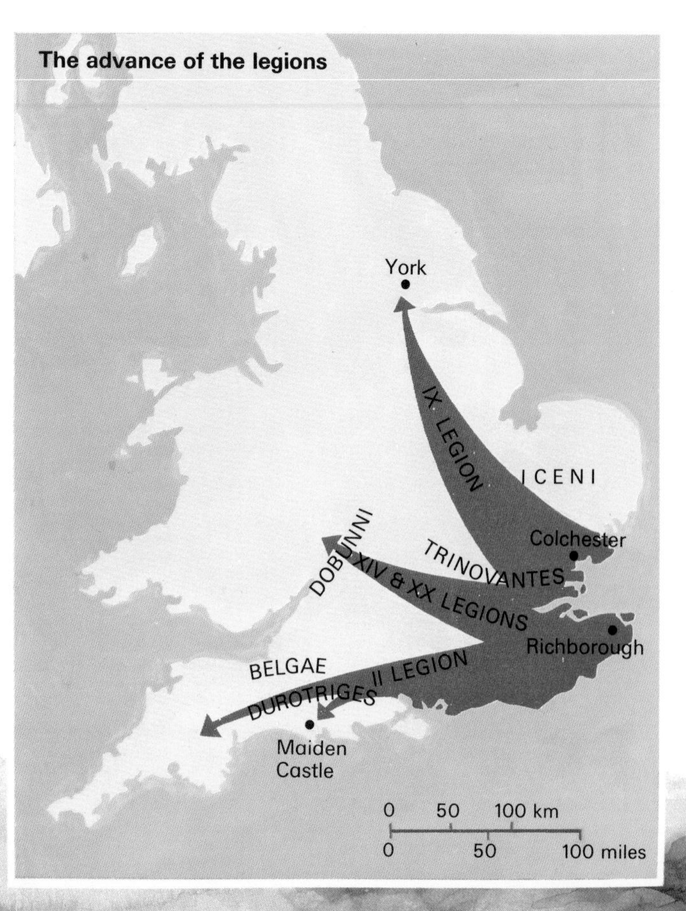

Aulus Plautius brought his invasion forces in three fleets. He came ashore at Richborough, a huge natural harbour safe from wind and tide, and only a few miles north of the beach chosen by Julius Caesar. On Richborough Hill he set his base camp and from there the Legions pushed forward.

The Ninth thrust north through the land of the Trinovantes and the Iceni to build the fortress at York. The Fourteenth and Twentieth together drove a road north-west through the Midlands and the Dobunni country towards the brooding hills of Wales. The Second, the Augusta, under the command of the future Emperor Vespasian, fought its way along the south coast, storming the great hill-forts of the Belgae and the Durotriges, including Maiden Castle. In four years half of southern Britain was firmly under Roman rule.

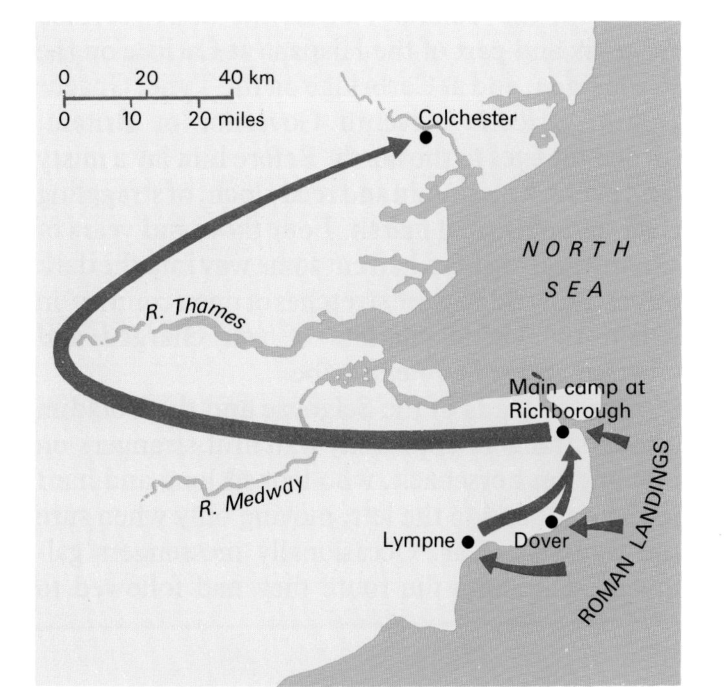

'In chariot fighting the Britains start by driving all over the field throwing javelins, and usually the terror inspired by the horses and the noise from the wheels is enough to throw their enemies' ranks into disorder. Then, after picking their way between the squadrons of their own cavalry, they leap down from their chariots and fight on foot. Meanwhile the charioteers retire a little way from the battle and hold the chariots in such a position that if their masters are hard pressed they have an easy way of retreating to their own lines. Plus they're able to combine the mobility of cavalry with the staying power of infantry. By daily training and practice they obtain such skill that even on a steep incline they are able to control their horses at full gallop and to check and turn them in seconds. They can run along the pole of the chariot, stand on the yoke and get back into the chariot as quick as lightning.'

Julius Caesar

left: Roman manoeuvres in south-west England 43 AD
below: The landing at Richborough

The invasion of the lowlands

Through the years that followed there were times of restless peace and bitter conflict but it was not until the late summer of AD 78, thirty-five years after Aulus Plautius first landed in southern Britain, that the man who would finish the job arrived. His name was Agricola. During his first year as Governor, he led his legions to victory over the tribes of Wales who had managed to hold out against the Roman invaders. In the following summer he crushed the last resistance in the north of England. The long conquest, begun at Richborough Hill was at last ended. The frontier of Roman Britain was secured from the Solway Firth in the west to the mouth of the River Tyne in the east and there was peace throughout the land.

With the Valeria Victrix, the newly formed Adiutrix and part of the Hispana at Carlisle on the River Eden, and at Corbridge on the Tyne, Gnaeus Julius Agricola, eleventh Governor of Britain, turned his eyes to the north. Before him lay a misty land of bleak mountain and reedy loch, of straggling river and of dismal marsh. Four thousand years of axe and grazing herd had cut some way into the dark forest. Now there were stretches of open country on which the Celtic chariots of war charged and wheeled and tribe fought tribe.

In the lands of the Selgovae and the Votadini armed strangers appeared; watchful strangers on foot and on horseback, who looked long and hard to the right and to the left, moving only when sure the way was clear. Occasionally messengers galloped back along the route they had followed to

A Roman army would move forward in the following formation. First came the advance guard lightly armed like those who scouted the way ahead. Some were archers. Behind them came a company of foot soldiers and cavalry ready to give support in the event of any sudden attack. Then there were the sappers and surveyors whose work it was to clear obstacles, level the ground where necessary, build the bridges and improve roads. After them came the high command. The General and his staff had a mounted escort and were closely followed by the cavalry and the siege machines. Next in line came the senior officers and their bodyguards and after them the legions each headed by its eagle and its standards. After the legions would come any mercenary forces and a rear guard made up of a strong contingent of heavy infantry and cavalry. The soldiers marched six abreast. They marched in their armour and in addition to his weapons and helmets each man carried equipment for pitching camp such as a saw and a pickaxe, cooking and eating utensils, a sickle, a basket, a bucket, a chain, a strap and food for at least three days.

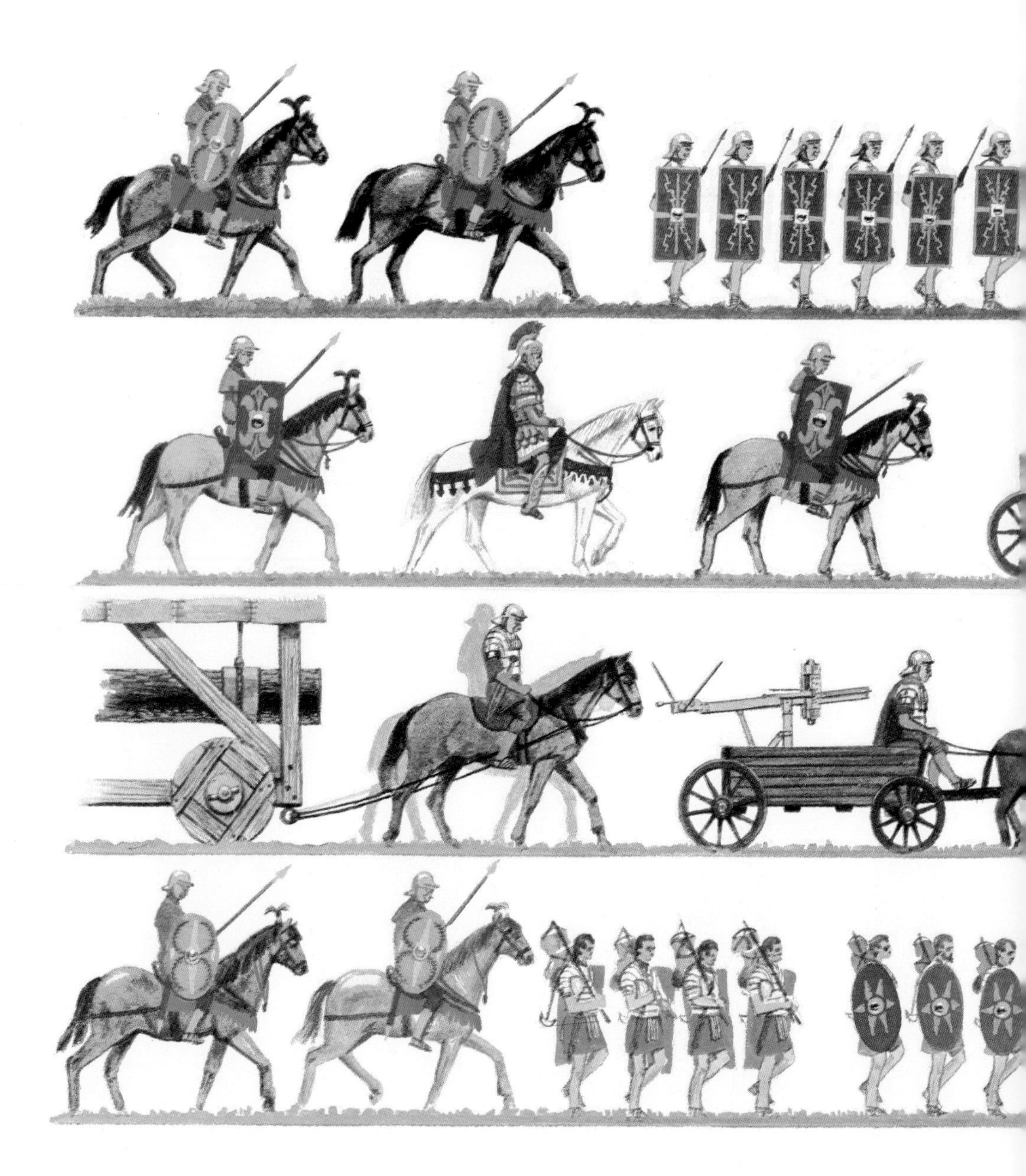

where a great column of armoured soldiers waited, rank upon rank, company upon company, a mile or more in length.

To the lowland tribes these dark newcomers did not seem like warriors. They stood in their neat ranks of six. They brought no chariots. Instead they stood meekly waiting some word of command from their officers. But when that word came and the whole column moved forward, the air was filled with the sound of marching and the hard ring of iron and there could be no doubt that these were the soldiers of a mighty army.

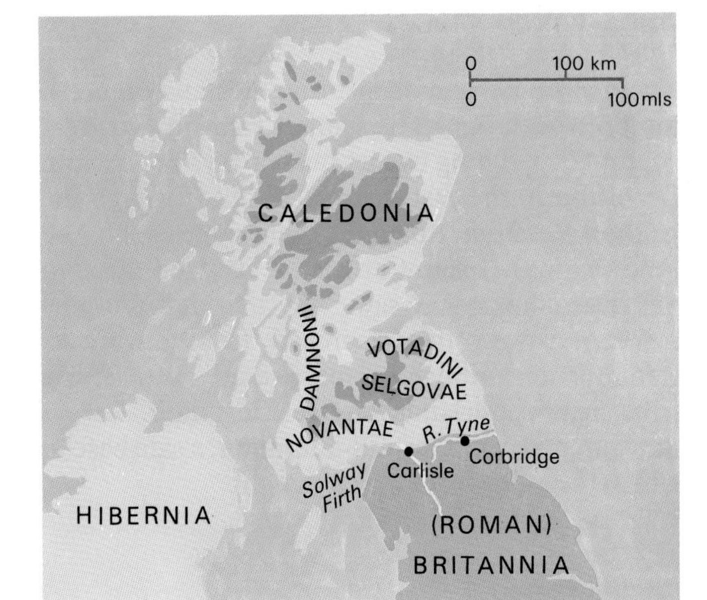

right: The Roman position by 78 AD

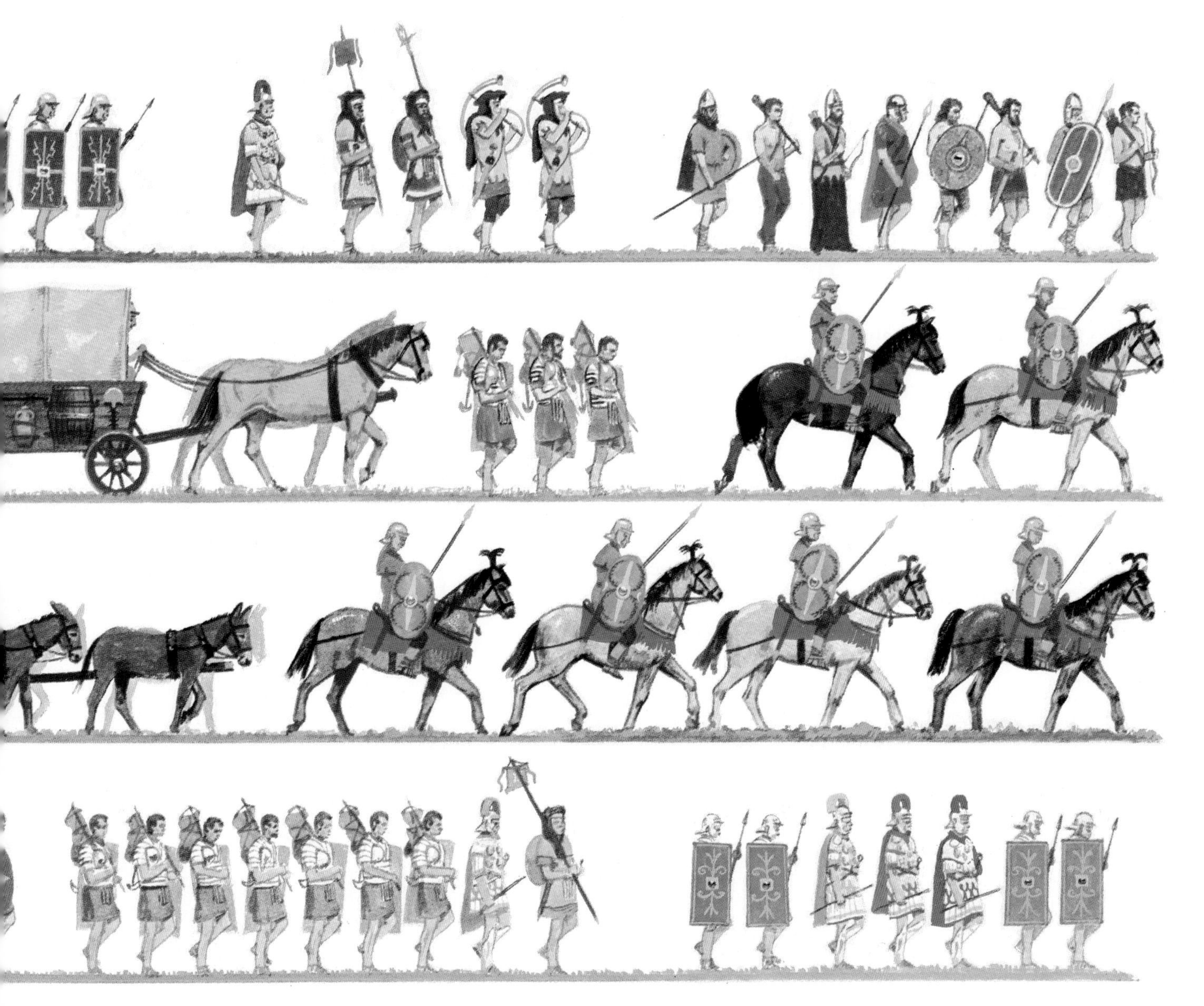

The campaign of AD 80–AD 82

The invasion began on a spring morning nineteen hundred years ago. The soldiers came in two great columns, marching twenty miles a day. Those from Corbridge in the east followed a route through the lands of Votadini, much the same route as the A68 follows today. From Carlisle the way led through Selgovae country the same way that the A74 now travels. Always they marched from daybreak, watchful for ambush or surprise attack from the tribesmen whose lands they were invading. Always they pitched camp by mid-afternoon, a safe base in which to rest or from which to fight.

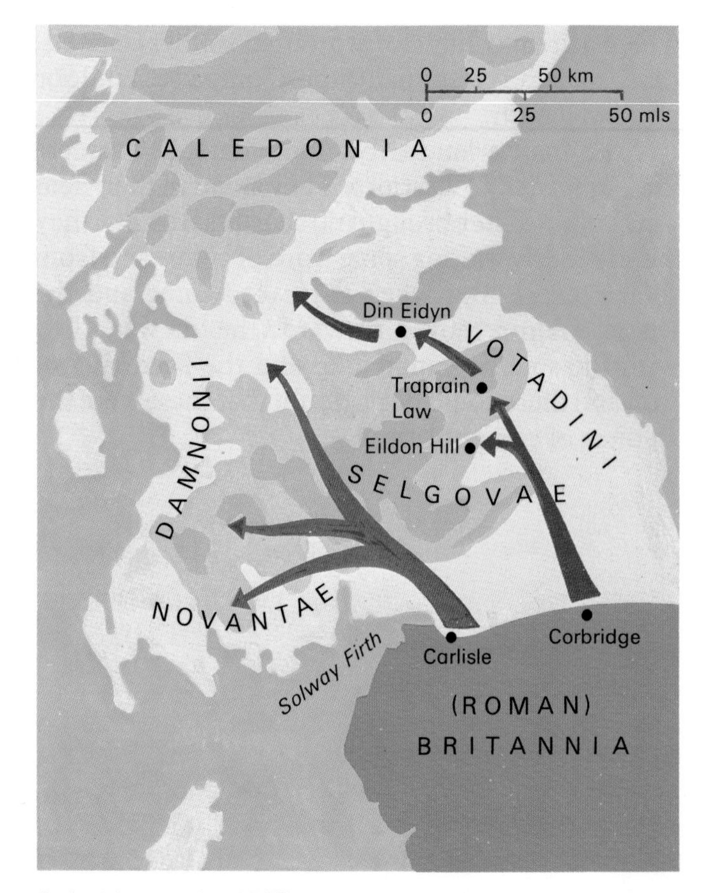

Agricola's campaign 80 AD

Pitching camp

From spring to autumn that year the Romans forced their way north through a bleak and hostile world, fording stream and bridging river, threading their way through marsh and forest. The wind-driven rain must have chilled the spirit of soldiers used to warmer places. And always there were the tribesmen.

The Votadini and Damnonii accepted, perhaps even welcomed, Roman rule and they were allowed to live on in their hilltop towns. The Votadini kept their capital on Traprain Law.

Because the Selgovae and the Novantae were more stubborn, Agricola forced them to submit. He marched on Eildon Hill, the great hilltop fortress of the Selgovae, a mile or two from where Selkirk now stands. There, five hundred or more Celtic round houses sheltered within its huge double circle of stone rampart and ditch. With the massive gates shut and the warrior Celts on the walls it would have been a daunting prospect to most attackers. But the Romans were masters of siege warfare and the taking of hillforts was little more than an exercise for which they had long practised.

Remains of a Roman entrenching tool, pick and turf cutter (**left**) and reconstructions of the finds

Pitching camp on Eildon Hill (**right**)

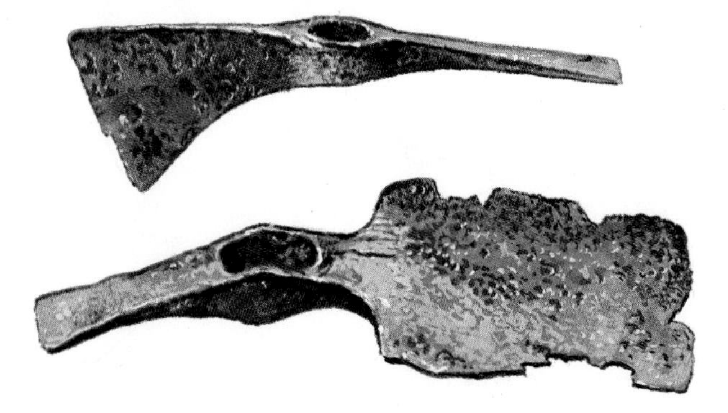

Under the direction of the sappers and the surveyors the ground was cleared and levelled by the legionaries. A deep ditch was dug to enclose the whole site and the soil from it was heaped up to form a solid rampart. Finally wooden stakes, brought by the soldiers, were driven into the top of the earth wall to give greater height. Only when the base was secure would the men pitch their tents and rest.

The attack on Eildon Hill

The Legions prepared carefully. There would be no hurried attack. From felled trees they built sheds to ward off enemy arrows and spears. Then the heavy artillery was moved into place and, where necessary, level emplacements were prepared. They had powerful catapults to hurl huge fire darts half a mile and mighty onagers to launch great rocks half the weight of a man. They had mobile ballistae to shower the enemy with heavy stones and giant crossbows called scorpions which fired iron-pointed bolts with deadly accuracy. With these weapons they pounded the fort until the defenders weakened. Only then did the Romans attempt to breach the defences, attacking suddenly and at several places at once. With fire and battering rams they struck at the massive gates. When the ramparts were broken the Legions poured through sparing no-one in pressing home their victory.

Because the Celtic tribes would not unite in arms against the invaders no force big enough to trouble the armies of Rome was put into the field. Agricola's men fought no major battles in southern Scotland.

A battering ram

above: Small catapults or 'Scorpions' fired bolts or balls

right: Catapult balls

Trimontium

As winter approached in the first year of fighting Agricola's two great columns met at Inveresk on the River Forth. By the end of the second year the Roman Empire had a new north-west frontier stretching from the Firth of Clyde to the Forth estuary. In the third, Agricola turned south again and to the west to finish his conquest of the Selgovae and the Novantae. Forts were built in key places. The largest was Trimontium at Newstead where it confronted the now deserted stronghold of Eildon Hill North. Roads too were built, on which army patrols could move more quickly and along which the conquered tribes could bring tributes of corn to their new masters. By AD 82 in south Scotland the war horn was silent, the chariot still. Throughout the land Pax Romana prevailed.

But not in the north. Beyond the new frontier there were fierce and hostile warriors always ready to raid and plunder the borderland of the Roman south. To Agricola the only safe frontier would be the northernmost coast of Scotland. Beyond it lay only the waters of the cold grey Atlantic. His legions once more prepared to move north. In AD 83 he crossed the Highland line.

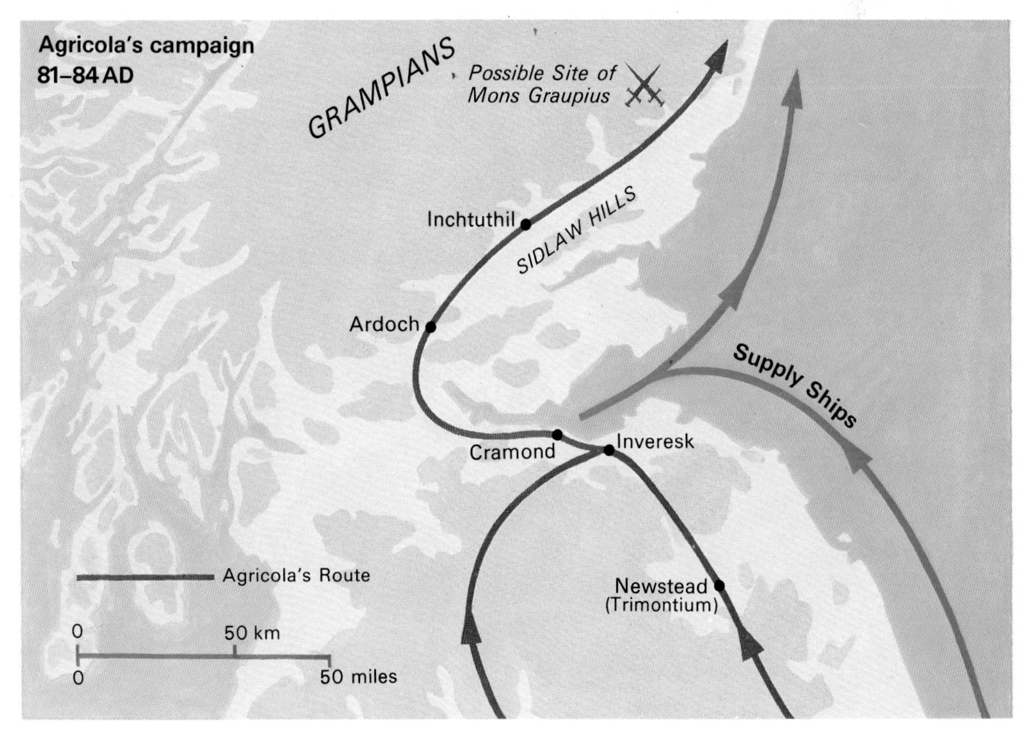

The misty north, with its barren mountains rising high above the tree line and its forest-filled valleys, was a bleak and unwelcoming place, harder even than the south. You can see from the map that one way led there, through Strath Allan by what are now Dunblane and Perth and on through the wide vale of Strathmore towards Stonehaven. Along that route Agricola took his men. On their right flank were the Sidlaw Hills and the sea beyond. Keeping pace with their march the Roman fleet coasted northwards bringing supplies and reinforcements, mounting commando raids on shore settlements. On their left flank lay the great range of Grampian Mountains cut deeply by glens and river valleys from which hostile warriors might suddenly attack.

The invasion of the Highlands

The Legions of Rome entered a land where the tribes had found some unity as one people. They were now in Caledonia. Agricola pushed forward with caution. His great army marched as three divisions some miles apart. It was a dangerous journey and what ground was won had to be secured. His plan was simple. As he advanced he plugged the open mouth of each glen with a fort – Bocastle in the valley of the River Teith, Dalingross in Strathearn, Fendock in Glen Almond, Inchtuthil in Strathtay, Gourdie in Glenshee and Cardean in the valley of the River Isla. One by one he closed every exit. The Caledonii were being trapped in their own barren highlands. Soon they would have to face the Roman Legions in pitched battle.

Attack on the Ninth Legion

Wary tribesmen who watched unseen from the foothill woodlands noted the weakness of one legion – the Hispana. It was well under strength with half its cohorts in the service of the Emperor Domitian in Germany. The Caledonii struck suddenly at night. They all but overran the Romans in Camp Victoria before being driven off by reinforcements from another division under the command of Agricola himself. With their lines of communication stretched and with the chill of a highland winter already in the air, the Legions turned and made their way south again, there to prepare for the next season's fighting.

below: How the glens were plugged

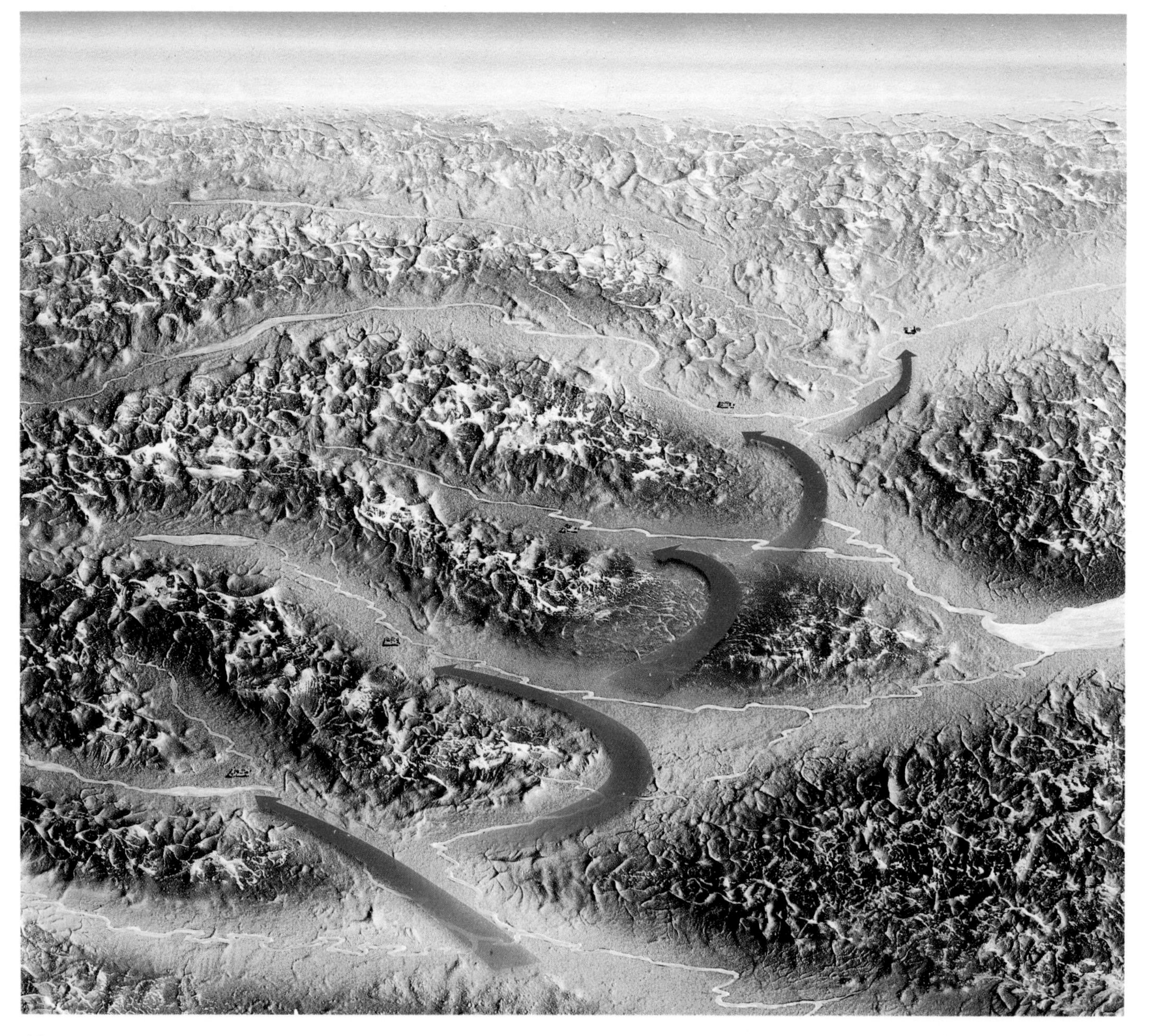

above: Roman warships and transports

The campaign of AD 84

In his seventh year as Governor of Roman Britain, Agricola embarked upon what was to be his last military campaign. By the same route as he had followed the previous year he led his army north again and, as before, he sent the fleet to raid the eastern coastline and to bring supplies. This time the Legions marched undivided as one force.

It was spring in AD 84 when this final thrust began but even today traces can be seen of the huge marching camps constructed by Agricola's men – at Carpow where they crossed the Tay, and at Oathlaw and Keithhock where they forded the South Esk and the North Esk on their way to where Stonehaven stands today. There they pitched camp at Raedykes before crossing the Dee at Normandykes and swinging north-west around the Grampian foothills. On through Aberdeenshire and Banffshire the great column marched, setting its camps at Kintore and Durno, at the Wells of Ythan and within sight of Spey Bay at Muiryfold about two miles from Keith and ten from the coast. They were almost at the Moray Firth and only fifty miles of easy country lay between the Roman Army and the mouth of the Great Glen. The trap had almost closed.

Calgacus

Now was the time for the Caledonii to face the might of Rome or be imprisoned in their own mountains. From round house and homestead, from dun and broch, they flocked to the call of one man, the first inhabitant of Scotland whose name we know – Calgacus. The Roman historian, Tacitus, records the substance of the speech he made to his warriors: 'We, the most distant dwellers upon the earth, the last of the free, have been shielded until now by our remoteness and by the obscurity which has shrouded our name. Now, the farthest bounds of Britain lie open to our enemies. There are no more nations beyond us – only waves, and rocks, and the Romans. Pillagers of the world, they have exhausted the land by their indiscriminate plunder. East and west alike have failed to satisfy them. To robbery, butchery, and rapine, they give the lying name "government". They create a desert and call it peace. Which will you choose – to follow me into battle, or to submit to taxation, labour in the mines and all the other tribulations of slavery? Whether you are to endure these forever or take a quick revenge, this battle must decide.' The tribes of Caledonia heard his words and, thirty thousand strong, they barred the Roman way.

Battle of Mons Graupius

It is not known where the battle of Mons Graupius took place but it is likely that it was near the place now called Fochabers on the River Spey, eight or so miles from the Roman Camp at Muiryfold. Agricola knew from his scouts that ahead of him the clans were gathering strength. He advanced cautiously with his forces already in battle array and the baggage train protected amongst them. It was the Roman custom to march in a state of constant battle readiness when in hostile conditions such as Agricola found in Moray.

In the sight of the assembling warriors the Legions prepared their camp between the rising ground and the sea. The cavalry, the advance guard and half the heavy infantry were halted facing the Caledonian position. The remainder were set to work erecting the defensive rampart of their square camp – each side fully half a mile in length. Agricola withdrew his men, company by company, behind the growing rampart wall until only the cavalry confronted the Celtic lines. When the front wall and ditch were complete the cavalry retired to their protection, keeping a wary eye on enemy movements until the camp was securely enclosed. With a heavy guard mounted, the soldiers pitched their tents and rested.

At first light the bugle summoned the Roman Army to the field in the formation planned by Agricola. The ranks were drawn up with their backs to the camp rampart. The auxiliaries were in the centre front and the cavalry on each wing. Behind were the soldiers of the Legions.

The cavalry battle

Facing the disciplined array of the Roman Army was the restless host of the Caledonii, every one a warrior impatient to hurl himself at the intruders, impatient too of command. Calgacus had placed his chariots to the front with the foot soldiers on the rising ground. Higher still were his reserves. He strained to hold them until the moment was right. At the blare of the war horn the chariots hurtled forward carrying the warlords against the ranks of the invaders. Weaving and wheeling with skill and courage they eluded the hail of Roman javelins and unleashed a volley of spears. With a furious energy they threw themselves on the enemy line. But the auxiliaries withstood the shock and, shield to shield, they held their ground. As the chariot attack weakened, Agricola countered with a cavalry charge, driving them from the field.

The infantry battle

Soon the foot-soldiers were locked in combat. The Caledonians, protected only by small round shields, swung their long swords slashing to right and to left. The legionaries, in their plate armour, stabbed and thrust with their short blades from behind an unbreakable wall of shields. Slowly but certainly the steady pressure of the solid Roman front pushed back the Caledonian centre. As Calgacus summoned his reserves from the high ground to steady the line, Agricola unleashed his main force of cavalry and the Caledonian ranks were broken. By mid-afternoon the battle had become a slaughter and the defeated tribes fled to the safety of the forests, where those Romans who pursued them too eagerly risked ambush. In this last battle Agricola was triumphant. The north had been subdued. All Britain was under Roman rule.

Or at least, that is how it must have seemed to the victorious Legions as they paraded through the newly conquered land. Thirty forts had been built in key places to control the tribes further south and more than thirteen hundred miles of good road laid to make troop movements quicker and easier. It was late in the summer, however, and no time remained to establish police-posts in Caledonia to maintain Roman order. That must wait for the next season's campaign. In the meantime, Agricola marched south again to his winter quarters.

Recall of Agricola

During the winter of AD 84 a decision was taken in Rome by the Emperor Domitian which it could be argued, was the greatest blunder in the history of Roman Britain. Just a season's campaign from what may have been a final step in establishing complete Roman control in Scotland, Agricola was recalled to Rome to be honoured for his services to the Empire. Tacitus says that Domitian was jealous of Agricola's success and popularity. Many modern historians believe that the enormous cost of Agricola's campaigns was beginning to worry the Emperor. Or perhaps he overestimated the defeat inflicted on the tribesmen. Within two years of the battle of Mons Graupius he had withdrawn the

above: Domitian's head on a coin

right: A Caledonian warrior

Second, Adiutrix, to Pannonia on the Danube. In these two years the Caledonians had lain still in their mountains, catching their breath, nursing their anger. Now Britain was left with only three legions. At Chester, the Valeria Victrix controlled North Wales and the Western Pennines. At Caerleon, just north of the Bristol Channel, the Augusta commanded the South West and South Wales. The Hispana, now withdrawn to York from the unfinished fortress of Pinnata Castra at Inchtuthil, was expected to patrol all of Eastern Britain from Strathmore to the far south.

The destruction of the northern forts

As the years passed, further withdrawals of Roman soldiers for service overseas weakened the garrison in Britain. In the same years something else was happening. Far to the north in the hills beyond the Tay a new generation of Caledonians was growing to manhood. Those who had been boys at Mons Graupius were now men, ready for the battle line, raised in the tradition of revenge. Within one decade of Agricola's greatest triumph they had come out of their wilderness of mountain, forest and marsh to attack and to destroy the northern forts. Within two they had struck further south and, aided by the restless Selgovae, burned to the ground the forts of Dalswinton and Glenlocher.

The Ninth Legion

Even the mighty Trimontium fell, and others too, all built to impose the Roman rule. During this time of northern vengeance, the Ninth, Hispana, twice before the victim of crushing encounters with the Britons – at Camp Victoria and against Boudicca – marched north from York in full battle order to the relief of the stricken garrisons. They were never heard of again. Some people believe that the Ninth was massacred by the northern tribes. Some argue that the records of the legion, and not its soldiers were lost. Evidence suggests that officers of the Ninth were transferred to other legions and that their extremely slow rate of promotion indicates a past disgrace. The mystery remains.

'Part of a bronze diploma from the time of Hadrian. Diplomas were given to auxiliary soldiers on completion of 25 years service in the army.

Retreat of the Romans

In the face of these fierce counter raids, the Romans fell back to the position they had held at the time Agricola had first come to Britain. Once more the frontier ran from the Solway in the west to the Tyne in the east. But this time it was to be different. This time there would be no forward movement. The new Emperor, Hadrian, had decided that the occupation of what is now Scotland was simply not worth the effort and expense.

Hadrian's Wall

In AD 118 Pompeius Falco was appointed Governor of Britain and within a year, at the command of Hadrian he had begun preparations for what was to be a tremendous feat of engineering. Tribesmen in the borderland watched with interest, and perhaps some concern, this new kind of Roman activity. All along the frontier teams of surveyors were taking measurements and striking lines of direction from point to point. By the spring of AD 120, what some may have guessed at and feared, was already happening. A huge work force, perhaps twenty thousand strong, was engaged in a massive construction operation. Stone quarries were opened and lime pits dug. Well shafts were sunk and new works roads laid. Men and mules dragged great loads of stone and lime, toiling team after team in an endless chain. The air was filled with the smoke and dust of kiln and quarry and rang to the sound of the stonemason's hammer. And far out in front were the patrols of the heavily armed soldiers who kept a watchful guard, protecting the work and the workers from the unwelcome attentions of native warriors.

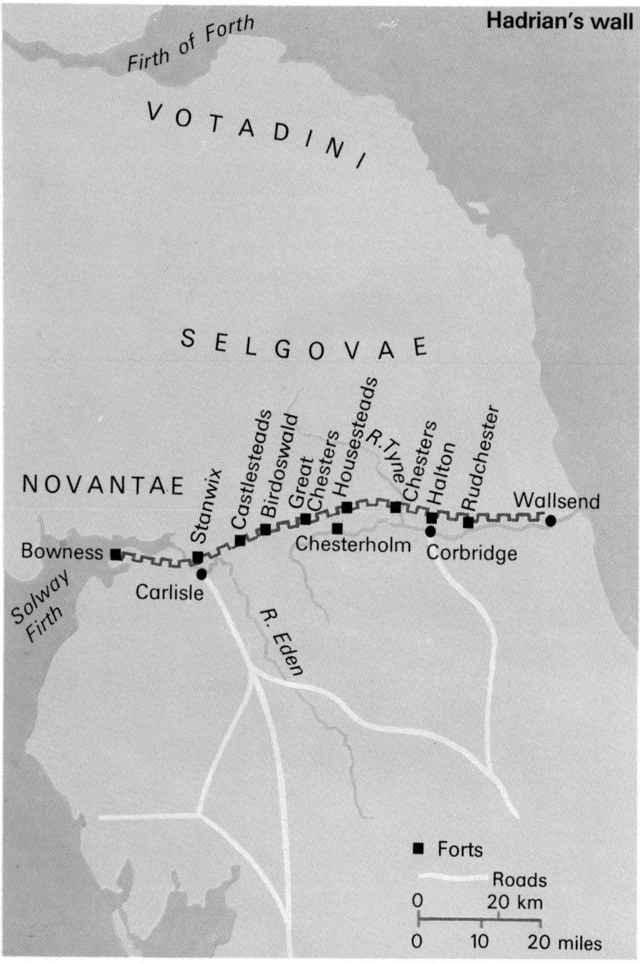

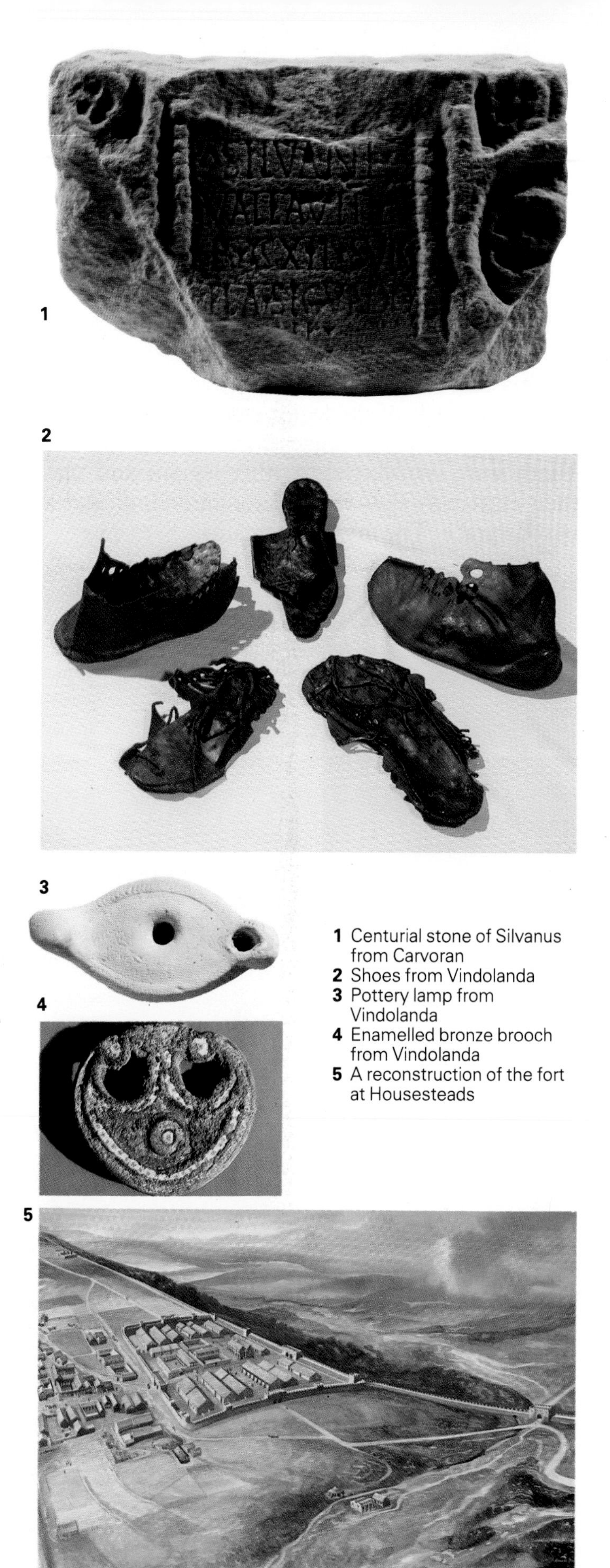

1 Centurial stone of Silvanus from Carvoran
2 Shoes from Vindolanda
3 Pottery lamp from Vindolanda
4 Enamelled bronze brooch from Vindolanda
5 A reconstruction of the fort at Housesteads

Building the Wall

As far as the eye could see to the east and to the west, legionaries and marines laboured long and hard. Across the land they laid mile upon mile of foundation stones, matched metre for metre on each side by a deep wide ditch. At intervals of a third of a mile rose the walls of towers and mile castles, camps and forts to be joined by one great rampart of stone, more than six metres high and three in breadth. When Hadrian's mighty wall was finished it would stretch over seventy miles from coast to coast, a tribute in stone and sweat to the fierce determination of the tribes it was designed to keep out – the Selgovae, the Novantae and the Caledonii. But it was more than just a wall. The Roman engineers had designed a whole system of defensive weaponry, able to detect, withstand and strike back. Sentries in the watch towers would spot the would-be intruders and alert the nearest soldiers who would resist the attack in its initial stages. Meanwhile the signal towers would relay the alarm to bring reinforcements with all speed along the road which ran behind the wall. In very little time a powerful force of cavalry could sweep out through the gates to engage the enemy in the field. So fast did the wall defences react that within one hour of an alert, two thousand trained infantrymen and cavalry could confront attackers wherever they might choose to strike. Hadrian's wall was a mighty obstacle to raiders from the north. The frontier was at last secure, the most strongly defended in all the Roman Empire.

Antoninus Pius and the campaigns of AD 141 and 142

But things were not to remain that way for long. In only twenty years a new Emperor had succeeded Hadrian and with him came new ideas. Antoninus Pius took office in AD 138 and within three years the Legions once more struck north, in two columns out of Carlisle and Corbridge, just as they had done under Agricola sixty years before. In two seasons' hard fighting they pushed up into Strathmore. But that was to be as far as they would go. An army, smaller when it set out than Agricola's and made smaller still by casualties in the field and garrison duties in places already taken, was simply not up to a long campaign in the north. Instead the surveyors, the engineers and the men of the Legions set to work once more.

right: Remains of the Antonine wall today

The Antonine Wall

Across the waistline of Scotland the Legions built the Antonine Wall. It stretched from Bridgeness on the Forth estuary to Old Kilpatrick on the Firth of Clyde, thirty-seven miles in all. On a four-metre wide foundation of rough stone held in place between two lines of dressed kerbing, they raised the wall, not in stone, but in blocks of turf laid like bricks. When finished it stood six metres high including its heavy wooden battlements – a great rampart joining nineteen forts built at two mile intervals. In front was a gaping ditch more than twelve metres wide and four deep. Behind ran the Military Way, a road on which troops could move quickly and easily. The Roman sentries from their cold high perch on the rampart walk, could see the high ground of the Kilsyth Hills and the Campsie Fells beyond which rose the brooding mountains of the northern tribes. For those Caledonians who ventured south with their minds set on plunder there was now a daunting barrier stretching mile upon mile, from coast to coast. The frontier had moved north once more.

An uneasy peace

In the face of repeated attacks upon it and perhaps for other reasons, the Antonine Wall was abandoned within a mere twenty years of its construction. Hadrian's Wall became once again the frontier and the subject of fierce raids.

In AD 209, under the command of the Emperor Severus, the Legions marched again to quell the unruly north, this time so vigorously that the submission they took by force lasted for nearly a century. During this period the Romans held their wall and guarded their territory beyond, while the Caledonians remained in their forbidding mountains. It was an uneasy peace.

And so it went on for another century or more. Southern Britain accepted Roman rule and culture but the north, the place we now call Scotland, remained restless and unsettled. Sometimes there was outright conflict and sometimes a brooding quiet, but never was there peace as in the south. Some tribes were hostile and some tribes were co-operative, but never were the people Romanized as in the south. When, after four hundred years in Britain, the Legions finally departed the contribution they had made to Scotland was a small one. They had come as invaders but had not settled. They had come as conquerors but had not subdued. Only their military roads and empty forts remained as monuments to their time in this land, to speed travellers on their journeys and to shelter the homeless. Only their secrets of glassmaking and their better ways of metalcraft were passed down to be added to the skills of the north Britons. Unlike the south there were no Roman towns nor Roman laws, no Roman government nor Roman economy – just a land and its peoples living on their hilltops and crannogs, in their brochs and duns as they had been when the Eagles of Rome first made their great advance under Agricola. Unable to take the north by force the Romans had separated it from the south by a mighty wall of stone. Perhaps for that reason as much as any in history Britain came to be divided into two Kingdoms, one of which would be called Scotland.

Worksection

The Romans

Understand Your Work

The Romans Arrive

1 How long had Scotland been Celtic before the Romans arrived in Britain?
2 What was happening in Boulogne in AD 43? Can you find this port on a modern map?
3 Who led the inconclusive earlier invasions of Britain?
4 Where did Aulus Plautius land his invasion forces?
5 Why was this place a good choice for the landing?
6 In what direction did the Romans advance?
7 How long did the Romans take to subdue the southern half of England? The whole of England?
8 Who completed the conquest of England?

The Legions

1 Which legions invaded Britain in AD 43?
2 Find on a map the places they came from.
3 How many men made up a legion at this time?
4 How many men were commanded by a centurion?
5 What protection did a foot-soldier of the legions wear and carry?
6 With what weapons was he equipped?
7 How many cavalry were there in a legion?
8 In what ways was an auxiliary different from a legionary?
9 Look at the picture on page 33. Describe how a legion was made up.

The Invaders

1 When did the Romans enter what is now Scotland?
2 Who led the attack?
3 Which legions marched north?
4 What kind of countryside did they enter?
5 In whose lands were they first sighted?
6 What troops were at the head of the Roman column?
7 Where did the General and high command ride?
8 Who marched at the head of each legion?
9 Who formed the rear guard of the column?
10 How were the soldiers dressed and equipped?
11 Look at the map on page 37. Which Celtic tribes would the Romans first encounter in Scotland?

The First Campaign

1 By what routes did the Romans enter Scotland?
2 What depressed the Romans?
3 Against whom were they always on their guard?
4 How did the Romans find shelter and rest during their marches?
5 Who directed the building of the marching forts?
6 In the Lowlands, which tribes accepted Roman rule and which resisted?
7 Which great hill fort of the Selgovae did Agricola take?
8 In AD 82, by the end of the first campaign, where was the Roman frontier?
9 Describe the tools in the pictures on pages 38 & 39.

Attack on Eildon Hill?

1 Where is Eildon Hill?
2 How was the hillfort there protected?
3 How many houses did it contain?
4 How did the Romans protect themselves from Celtic arrows and spears?
5 What special weapons did the legions use against hillforts?
6 What was the first stage of the attack?
7 When did they attempt to storm the walls?
8 How did they break through?
9 Imagine you are inside the fort at Trimontium. Describe what you see.

The Highlands Invasion

1 What route did Agricola follow?
2 How were his troops supplied and supported?
3 How did the Romans secure each glen as they passed? Find these places on the map.
4 What was Agricola doing to the Caledonii?
5 What happened to the Ninth Legion during this campaign?
6 What caused Agricola to break off fighting and return to base in AD 83?
7 When the legions returned the following spring, how did their marching order differ from the previous year?
8 Where had the Romans reached when their trap was almost closed?
9 Who led the Caledonian resistance?
10 Find on your map the place where the battle of Mons Graupius took place.
11 How did the Romans arrange their men when marching in battle array?
12 How did the Caledonian forces differ from the Roman army?
13 How did Agricola finally turn the battle in favour of the Romans?
14 What could have happened to the Romans who chased the Caledonians too far?
15 Look at the ships on page 43. What are the differences between the warship and the transport?

Retreat of the Romans

1 What mistake did the Roman Emperor Domitian make which led to the loss of the north?
2 How was the Roman garrison in Britain weakened?
3 When and how did the Caledonians strike back?
4 What may have happened to the Ninth Legion during this time?
5 What happened to the Roman frontier because of the fierce attacks by the tribes?
6 Which major Roman forts were overrun?
7 Which Lowland tribe helped the Caledonii?
8 What work did the Emperor Hadrian command that the new Governor Pompeius Falco should carry out?

Hadrian's Wall

1 In what year was the wall begun?
2 What was the first stage in preparing for the construction of the wall?
3 How large a workforce was needed?
4 How were stone, timber and other building materials found?
5 How were the work gangs protected from the tribesmen?
6 How long was the wall?
7 How were the defensive towers and forts spread along the wall?
8 How did the garrison strike back if the wall came under attack?
9 Imagine you are one of the soldiers in the picture on page 49. Explain what is going on.

The Antonine Wall

1 Why did the northern invasion of AD 141–2 fail to conquer the whole of Scotland?
2 Where did the Romans fix the frontier?
3 How did the Antonine Wall differ from Hadrian's Wall?
4 For how long did the Romans use this wall as their northern frontier?
5 What caused them to abandon it?
6 To where did the Romans withdraw the frontier?
7 Who led the final northern advance of the Romans?
8 How successful was this campaign?
9 How did the effects the Romans had on Scotland differ from the effects they had on England?
10 Imagine you are the soldier in the picture on page 51. Tell the story of what is happening.

Use Your Imagination

1 Why do you think some Roman armour was made of loosely jointed strips and plates?

2 Why was a rectangular shield a better shape than say a round one for the foot soldiers? (Think of them standing side by side.)

3 When the Roman soldiers forded a fast flowing stream half the cavalry formed a line on horseback upstream and the other half downstream of the column as it waded across. Why do you think they did this?

4 Man for man the Celtic warriors had few equals as fighters. Why do you think the Roman army was able to defeat them quite easily?

5 The Roman fort had four gates making it easy for the soldiers to get out and form up in battle order quickly. Why do you think the Roman army used forts like this?

6 See if you can design a gateway for a Roman marching fort which would make surprise attack more difficult but still allow the Romans to get out quickly.

7 What reasons do you think the Romans might have for giving up the struggle in the wild barren lands of the north?

8 The Roman pilum was a light throwing spear with a weak easily bent section near the point. Why do you think it was made in this way?

9 Hadrian's Wall, like any other wall, could be climbed or broken down by attackers. How did the Romans stop this happening?

10 The Romans could defeat the Celts easily so long as they did not band together in one mighty army. What might they do to make sure this did not happen?

11 How do you think the roads the Romans built helped them to keep the country under control?

Further Work

1 Imagine you are a Celt. From your hiding place in the rocks you see the Romans arriving on the beach, lining up all neat and tidy and taking orders from officers in fancy dress! Knowing what the wild fearless warriors in your tribe are like what might you think of the Romans, at first sight? Do they look a dangerous enemy? Write down a note of the things you might tell the tribe when you report what you have seen.

2 The Celtic warriors were great and brave fighters. They were proud of their strength and courage. The Celtic forces depended on their great heroes. Celts fought for themselves.
A Roman army was well organised and soldiers usually obeyed their officers' orders without thinking. They fought and thought as one unit under the direction of their general. Romans fought for Rome.
Write the speech which you would deliver either to the Celts or to the Romans before battle. Choose which you prefer.

3 The horses of ancient Scotland were too small and not strong enough to support a fully equipped warrior. It would take two such ponies! (This was a problem faced also by the Celts when transporting heavy goods.) How do you think a warrior might use two ponies to carry him in battle? Make a drawing of your idea, with notes to explain its special features.

4 When a wall is used to protect a frontier it is too long to be guarded everywhere. It is designed to slow down attacks until the defenders can get to the trouble spot in strength. Imagine you have to build such a defence against wild tribesmen using only materials easily found. Work out a system which will –
   1 Slow the attackers
   2 Permit the defenders to discover the attack and raise the alarm
   3 Make it possible to bring up reinforcements quickly enough.

5 Romans on duty on the cold northern frontier must have longed to be at home in the sunny warmth. As they stood guard they would compare the misery of sleet, wind, and desolate country with their own land. Can you write down some of the thoughts they might have had about home and family, about bitter cold and savage tribesmen? You could make this into a poem.

After the Romans

Last of the legions

It was about the year AD 410 that the last of the legions left Britain. Rome was gathering her strength for a final desperate stand. Invading hosts from Germany had overrun the Empire and were now hammering on the city walls. The people living in the cold craggy land north of Hadrian's wall went about the business of survival much as they had always done. What changes the Roman years had brought showed mainly in the kingdoms south of the crumbling rampart and burnt-out forts of the Antonine Wall.

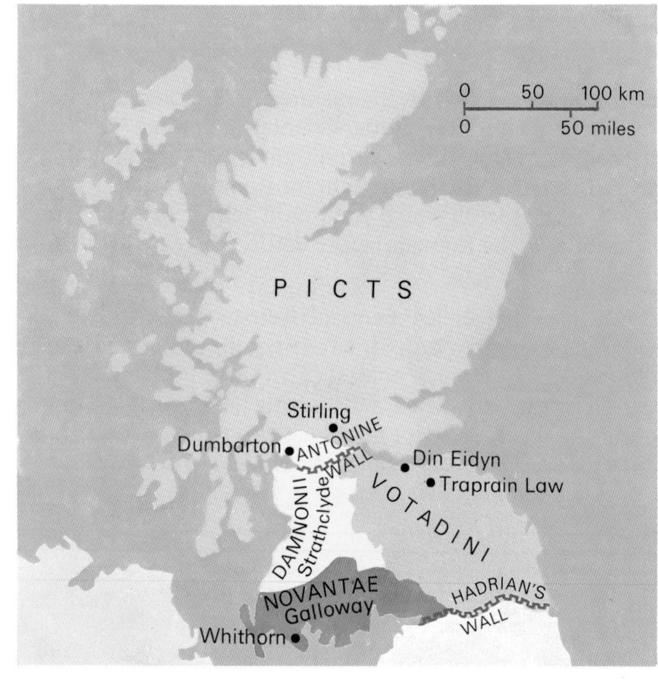

below: Remains of the chapel of St. Ninian, founded in the 9th century and rebuilt in the 11th

above: The location of the Celtic tribes 410 AD
right: Tribal fortress at Din Eidyn

The Votadini

The Votadini, the first of the few tribes to have offered any friendship to the Roman intruders, continued to raise their crops and tend their herds, to forge their tools and craft their ornaments. They still lived in round farmhouses but their fields, now turned by the plough, were longer and straighter. Their great tribal capital and fortress still stood on Traprain Law but now they had two more strongholds, at Din Eidyn (Edinburgh) and Stirling.

The Novantae

To the south-west, in Galloway, was another kingdom of Britons, where Cole Hen, whom some have identified as 'Old King Cole', ruled the Novantae and founded a line of kings. Here the people of the tribe still lived in their crannog dwellings on their lochs, tending their lonely farmsteads. Here too, perhaps before the Roman withdrawal, Scotland's first saint established his first church. His name was Niniavus and he was a Roman Briton from Carlisle, a bishop trained in the Roman Christian faith. Because he built his church in stone, washed white with lime, a style very unusual to the local people, it came to be known as Candida Casa – the White House. From here St. Ninian carried the message of Christianity amongst the northern peoples. To this day, the town which stands on the site of St. Ninian's church bears the name Whithorn, which comes from the old Northumbrian words 'hwit aern' meaning 'White House'.

The Damnonii

North of the Novantian lands lay the kingdom of the Damnonii, stretching up to Loch Lomond and eastwards almost to Stirling. It was called Strathclyde and its capital was Dumbarton.

The Picts

North of these British peoples and beyond the Antonine Wall were the Caledonii and other tribes who for so long had fiercely opposed the might of Rome. To all of them the Romans had given one name, a nickname intended to make fun of an enemy who tattooed their skin. They called them by a Latin word meaning 'painted people', a name that would ring loudly and clearly across the centuries. They called them the Picts. The Picts were made up from all those settlers who for centuries had made their great journeys over land and sea to find a new homeland in Scotland – those very first hunters with their simple weapons and traps, the farmers who hacked clearings in the dark forests with axes of stone, the men of bronze who brought metalcraft and trade, the warlike Celts with their mastery of iron.

Damnonii

Novantae

Votadini **Pict**

The great alliance

When the Romans began to withdraw from north Britain the Picts were divided in two groups living north and south of the high ground called the Mounth which cuts across north-east Scotland just below the River Dee. Like all the other peoples of Britain, they were farmers, first and foremost. They won their food from the land and life was hard. Their herds and flocks had to be protected from lynx and bear, but most of all from the prowling wolf. In these rugged conditions the Picts forced a living from the soil, hunting and fishing to make good what their farms could not provide.

Even before the Romans left, raiding parties from Ireland had been striking at the western edge of south Britain. The Picts looked south to a province rich in plunder, a treasure house crammed with silver and gold, slaves and cattle. And as they looked they nursed an anger fed by three and a half centuries of Roman domination and oppression. Out of their resentment and at the prospect of such plunder a plan was forged. The Irish, the Picts and the Saxons from the continent would unite in a great alliance of tribes against the Romans.

Never before had such a plan been dared. Its success would depend on surprise and no warning must be allowed to reach the Romans. The Arcani, which was a kind of Roman secret service, was bribed to report nothing. And so the garrison never suspected that the warrior chieftains of the northern tribes were mustering their men and moving quietly south. In Ireland powerful fleets of hide-covered curraghs raised their red sails and slipped out from their havens to bear eastwards for Britain. To the unguarded coastline of Yorkshire came other craft, their high prows cutting white furrows through the water. They were manned perhaps by Saxons, whose main fleet was further south, or perhaps by the Picts themselves coasting down past the eastern end of the wall.

No hint of the approaching danger reached the defenders. The timing was exact. By land and by sea, the raiders struck with lightning speed. The Picts swept down on the wall and carried it on their first rush. The ships of their allies crunched on to the shingle and sand of unprotected beaches up and down both coastlines and the seaborne warriors

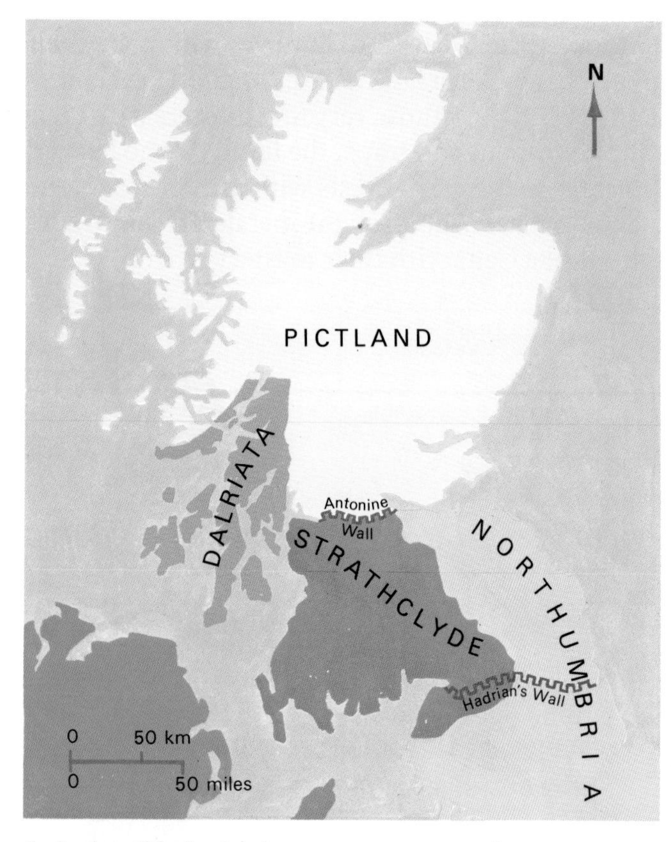

At the time of the Legions' departure the land we now call Scotland was shared by the Picts to the north and the Britons to the south. Their territories were divided by the ruins of the Antonine Wall.

thrust inwards. Too late the warning beacons were lit and the alarm raised.

The first word to reach Fullofaudes, Commander-in-Chief of the Roman army in Britain was of the disaster at the wall. Not realizing the tremendous weight and speed of the Pictish advance, he rushed from his headquarters at York to restore order amongst the garrison. He was ambushed and captured before reaching his destination. Nectaridus, Commander-in-Chief of the coastal region, was killed in an early engagement.

With the loss of two generals the Roman army retreated in confusion before the surging advance of the great alliance. In a campaign of startling speed the tribal forces raced southwards. The whole country was ablaze and London lay under siege. Victory was complete.

Their vengeance satisfied, the allies turned to plunder, and picked the province clean. By the time Roman reinforcements arrived under Theodosius the campaign was over. The armies of the alliance had broken up with warrior bands taking what booty they could seize as they returned northwards.

In that northern alliance the Irish had found common cause with the Picts and a link was forged with Pictland which would lead, one day, to the single most important event in Scottish history.

Perhaps for the part they played in that campaign the Irish were given lands on the west coast of Pictland in the area of Kintyre and Knapdale. In any case events were taking place in Ireland during the fifth century which caused settlers from what is now Antrim but was then known by the name of its people, the Dal Riata, to cross the North Channel and land on the Mull of Kintyre. Before the end of that century, Fergus Mor, King of the Dal Riata had forsaken his royal capital in Ireland and made a new kingdom in Kintyre. What makes this so important is that these Celts from Ireland were known also by another name, a nickname which meant 'raiders'. They were called the 'Scots'.

They settled quickly in the land that would one day bear their name. And they spread. Within half a century they occupied all of what is now Argyll and were in conflict with the Picts and the British Kingdom of Strathclyde.

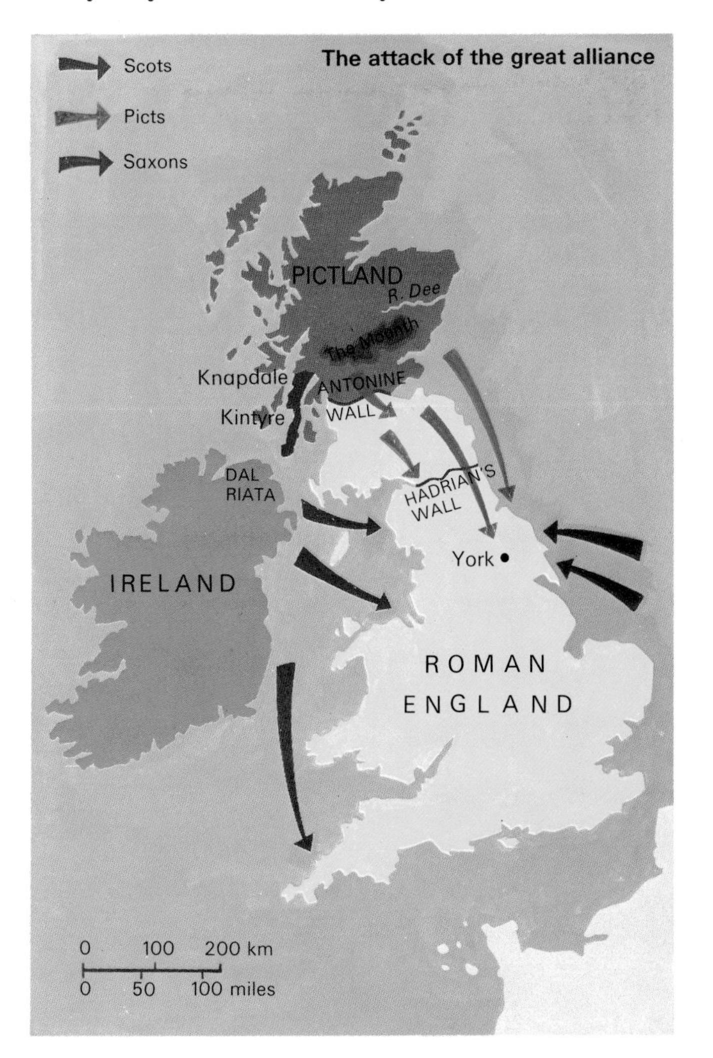

Pictish warrior on a stone from Rhynie in Aberdeenshire

The exile

To this new Dal Riata, in the year AD 563, there came a high-born man of the church. For what was said to be his part in causing civil war, this man had been exiled from his native Ireland. He set sail with twelve companions and eventually found a resting place on the little island of Hy just off the west coast of Mull. There they founded a monastery from which they carried Christian teaching to Scots and Picts alike. The island is better known to-day as Iona. The man was St. Columba.

Columba brought more than a religious message to Dal Riata. By his princely prestige and personality he strengthened the Scots' hold on their new kingdom against the pressures from Pict and Briton. By his statesmanship he helped to unite them under the rule of Aedan, the great grandson of Fergus Mor. By his influence and preaching he won the respect and friendship of Brude, King of all the Northern Picts and converted him to Christianity.

above: St. Columba **inset:** Iona

Life in Dal Riata

As in all Britain, the Scots raised crops and tended livestock. The common people lived in their hamlets and worked their farms. They paid tribute in the form of a food rent to the lord or king on whose lands they laboured. More than that, they were required to undertake military service both on land and sea. So important to this water-locked kingdom was naval power that from every twenty of these tiny hamlets, twenty-eight men were required for rowing service.

And after the long toil of the day, the evening hours would be spent around the hearth in the smoky warmth of their thatched dwellings. Here would be told the stories of great deeds, which became greater in the telling. And perhaps too would be heard the music of the harp, that instrument of antiquity best loved by the Celt, long before the skirl of the bagpipe drowned its rippling strings.

Vortigern's mistake

With the Legions no longer there to protect them the Roman Britons in the south had to fight for themselves. The leader who came forward to direct that fight was a man called Vortigern. Realizing that the South Britons were simply not strong enough to resist the fierce attackers from all sides, Vortigern paid for three shiploads of equally fierce warriors from the continent to settle in the area that is now Kent and from there to repel the Pictish pirates. The new defenders were Saxons. And it worked well for a time. Vortigern had used the same idea with success to defeat the attacks made by the Irish against the coast of North Wales, employing men from the Votadini to reinforce his defences.

In Kent, however, the success was shortlived. The Saxons themselves turned on the Britons and by AD 500 had occupied all but the west of England. What began by invitation ended as invasion. Vortigern had opened the gates and a flood not only of Saxons, but Angles and Jutes as well, poured into the land from across the North Sea.

The Angles

It was the Angles in particular who took the north-east of the country beyond the River Humber. There they established the Kingdom of Deira, what we would call Yorkshire. And they went further. They moved north supported by their ships and extended their territory towards the River Forth. They drove the Votadini from their great capital on Traprain Law.

Bernicia

This newly conquered land they called Bernicia and they fought hard to hold it in the face of fierce attacks by the neighbouring Britons. The men of the Votadini struck back again, from their capital and fortress of Din Eidyn in their new Kingdom of Gododdin. They pushed south into the heartland of Deira to confront the Angles at Catterick. But they were pushed back. Not even the mighty Aedan, King of Dal Riata could subdue these determined men of Northumbria, the name by which their combined Kingdoms of Deira and Bernicia came to be known. The Angles had come to stay and to spread. By 642 they had captured Din Eidyn and Stirling and so occupied Gododdin.

The four peoples

And so the four peoples – the Picts and Scots, the Britons and Angles, out of whom would grow a nation, first came to what one day would be Scotland. For more than three long centuries they shared its mountains and marshes, its rivers and valleys, often loud with the din of war, never free from the striving of men. They turned the meagre soil and raised their grain. They hunted on horseback and drove their herds to summer pasture.

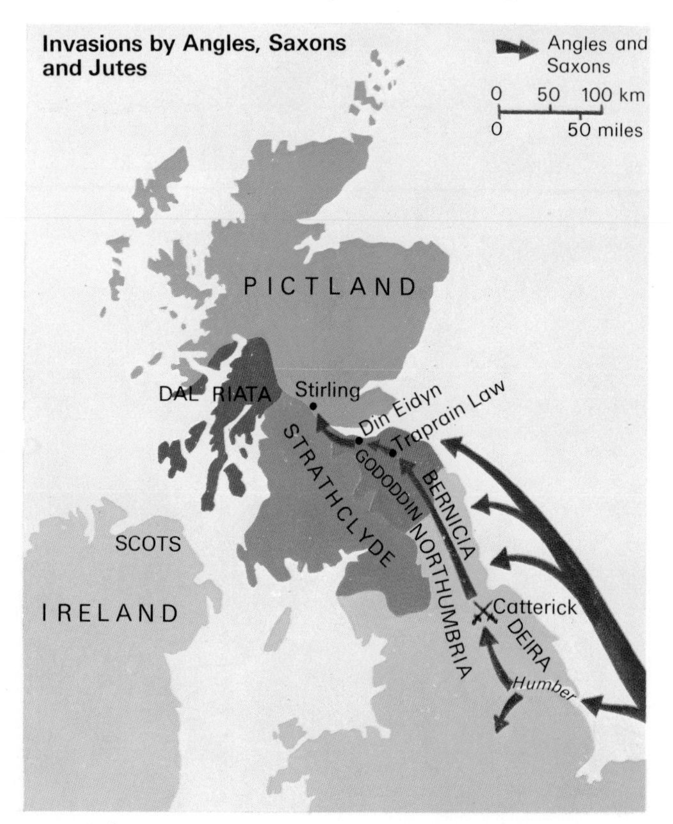

But they did more. They lifted their eyes to higher things, these Celtic peoples and the men of the new Bernicia. The Picts in the fastness of their mountain homes carved strange and beautiful pictures on slabs of stone: a goose with backswept glance, a prowling wolf, a stately deer, a heavy bull with lowered horns, a strutting stallion. And there were strange unearthly creatures too, and mystical designs of untold meaning. Though they left no written records, the Picts, in their pure and lovely sculpture, left images of how they lived: how the huntsman and the warrior dressed and what weapons they bore; what ships and chariots they used and the style of harness for their horses. What they did not show was brutality and man slaying man; no celebration of war, not even Christ crucified, only an empty cross and the angels weeping. Yet they were said to be a most ferocious and savage people, but then that was said by their enemies!

It was to his kin in Dal Riata that St. Columba first brought his Christian message and wherever his Celtic church served, it encouraged education and there were greater numbers of literate people than anywhere else in northern Europe. In the monasteries, artist monks laboured long hours grinding pigments and mixing colours, creating and drawing marvellous Celtic designs. These were applied with endless patience to decorate in glowing colour, manuscripts of breathtaking beauty. The greatest of them contains the four gospels and is from Iona. It was prepared for the Church of Kells in Ireland and is known simply as the Book of Kells.

Master craftsmen too, fashioned wonderful objects in gold and silver and bronze, bright with precious stones and brilliant enamels to adorn the Celtic Church.

below: The Brecbennoch of St. Columba, now called the 'Monymust Reliquary'.

Worksection

After the Romans

Understand Your Work

The Romans Leave

1. When did the legions finally leave Britain?
2. What caused the Romans to leave?
3. On which part of Scotland did the Romans leave their mark most clearly?
4. Where were the great tribal strongholds of the Votadini?
5. Find out what Pax Romana means?
6. Who was Cole Hen?
7. Who was St. Ninian?
8. What did his church in Galloway come to be called?
9. Where was the capital of the Damnonii?
10. Compare the map on page 54 with a modern map. Describe where the tribal borders ran using modern references.

The Picts

1. Who were the Picts?
2. What did the name mean?
3. What was their tribal name?
4. Where were their tribal lands?
5. How were the Picts divided? Find on your map the high ground which separated their lands.
6. Apart from farming, how did they find food?
7. Which wild animals threatened their livestock?
8. What attracted the Picts to raid southern Britain?

The Great Alliance

1. Who were the Arcani? See if you can find a modern English word which comes from this Roman word.
2. Why did the Arcani fail in their duty?
3. What was a curragh?
4. Who attacked the Yorkshire Coast?
5. What happened to the Roman Commander-in-chief?
6. Why was the attack so successful?
7. Were the Celts driven out by the Roman armies? Why did they leave?
8. Which peoples made the great alliance of tribes?
9. Try and draw a picture of a Pictish warrior from the illustration on page 57, and the other illustrations in the book.

Newcomers

1. Why may the Irish have been given lands in Pictland?
2. Where were these lands?
3. What was the name of the people who came?
4. Find on your map where they came from.
5. What is so important about these newcomers?
6. Who came to Dal Riata in 563 AD? Where did he settle?
7. What, apart from preaching, did he do for Dal Riata?
8. What important king did he make Christian?

Dal Riata

1. How did the Scots pay for the land they farmed in Dal Riata?
2. Apart from rent what service were they required to give?
3. How was the navy recruited?
4. How did the Scots find their daily living?
5. What pastimes did they enjoy around the hearths?
6. Which was the favourite instrument of the Celt?
7. Find on your map where Dal Riata had spread in the first fifty years.
8. Where is Iona?
9. Imagine that you are one of the characters in the picture on page 59. Describe your home.

The Angles and Saxons

1. How did Vortigern repel the Irish raid on the coast of North Wales?
2. What did he do to defeat the attacks made by the Pictish pirates on the south-east of England?
3. What went wrong with his scheme?
4. Which of the new tribes struck north?
5. What is the modern name for the kingdom of Deira?
6. Whom did the Angles drive from Traprain Law?
7. Find on your map the kingdoms of the Angles.
8. Who were the four peoples that occupied Scotland in the seventh century?
9. Look at the Angle warrior on page 60. How are his armour and weapons different from the Roman armour on page 33?

Ancient Scotland

1. What type of Pictish artwork still survives today?
2. What kind of things does it tell us about the Picts?
3. How did the Celtic Church help in education?
4. Who founded this Church?
5. What artistic work did the monks of the Celtic Church perform and for what purpose?
6. Where did they get their paints?
7. What is the best example of this work?
8. What other things of beauty did the Celtic craftsmen produce?
9. Describe any 3 of the objects on page 61.

Use Your Imagination

1. Why do you think crop fields became longer and straighter after the plough was introduced in Scotland?
2. Celtic wealth was counted in livestock and often increased by cattle raiding. Why do you think exchanging livestock for gold could sometimes be a better way to keep wealth?
3. How do you know that the Celtic people had by this time larger horses?
4. See if you can draw animals in the style of the Pictish sculptures.

5 What bargain do you think would have to be made with members of the Arcani before they would agree to help the tribes?

6 The allies were able to break through Hadrian's great defence because of surprise. Are there any other ways they could have done so? Any other tactics or tricks you can think of?

7 Having overrun the south why do you suppose the Celts did not remain there to govern and so create an empire?

8 Because of their nickname, the Dal Riata became what is called the eponymous tribe of Scotland. Can you think out what eponymous might mean? Check with your dictionary.

9 Make up a letter which Vortigern might have sent to persuade the Votadini or the Saxons to help defend the coast against raiders. (What would he offer, promise? What conditions would he lay down?)

10 Is there any way by which Vortigern could have made sure that his new Saxon allies led by Hengist and Horsa, would not turn against him? What might you do in his position?

Further Work

1 After looking carefully at the lovely patterns made by the Celtic monks, see if you can do the same kind of thing. With coloured pen or pencil draw your own initials to look like the work of the ancient Celtic monks. Be patient and work very carefully, then mount your finished designs so that they can be displayed.

2 As a Roman general, write a despatch to Rome explaining and excusing the crushing defeat of the Roman army in Britain by the tribes, and ask for help.

3 There would be stories of great deeds told by the warriors who had fought in the great alliance. Make up your own story of daring escape, or rescue, or desperate fight, or clever trick or . . .
When you have finished write another version of the very same event only, this time you are a Roman!

4 Visit a local museum and see what Celtic and Roman remains there are on exhibition. Find out where you can see Pictish stones with their elegant carvings.

The Coming of the Long Ships

To the north-east of Scotland and stretching five hundred miles up into the Arctic Circle was the land of the Norsemen. To-day we call it Scandinavia. Its ragged western coastline, more than sixteen hundred miles long, is gashed deeply with inlets and bays over whose shores tower hard bleak cliffs and mountains. Between the water's edge and the sharply rising ground there is a narrow margin of farmland. Here people looked to the sea for what the land could not provide. In sturdy rowing craft they fished their coastal waters and deep fjords. During the time when Scotland's four kingdoms were still disputing their uncertain frontiers, the Norsemen were finding it more and more difficult to feed their growing population.

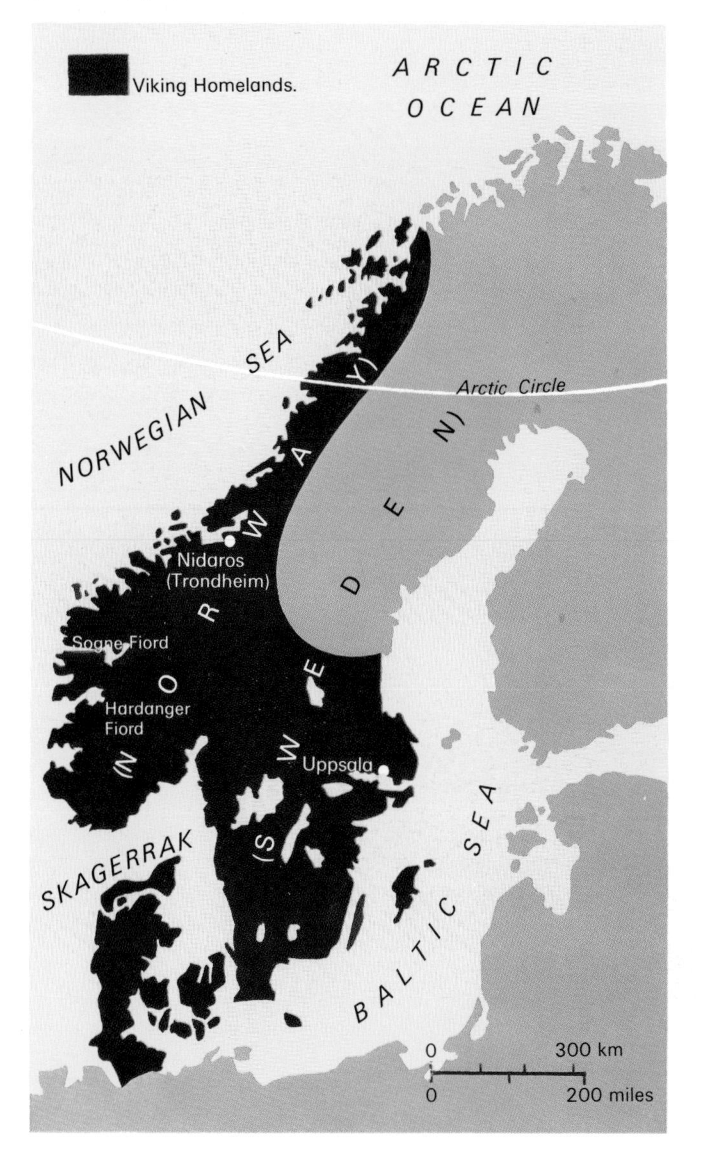

below: Remains of a Viking ship in the museum at Oslo

The Norsemen had already built excellent fishing boats and they had already shown the highest skills of seamanship as they navigated the dangerous rocks and swirling currents of their native coasts. Now they concentrated on improving the design of their boats. They added a deep keel – a massive single timber of solid oak, as much as eighteen metres in length, which reached down below the hull for almost half a metre. At each end an upcurved stem was added to form the bow and stern post. All along the keel's upper edge, cross ribs swept up, at metre intervals. To these were fastened strong oak planks, each overlapped by the one above and riveted to it with heavy iron nails clinched over square washers. The seams were sealed watertight with animal hair dipped in tar. This cladding of planks was bound and pegged to the ribs to form a slender and supple hull, low at the middle and sweeping high to bow and stern.

With the long straight blade of its keel to hold the course steady, the craft would resist any sideways push of the wind. The gathered force of the wind in the great square sail would be transmitted down the mast and through the keel block to drive the hull through the grey waters of the open sea. With ships like that the masters of the fjord became masters of the ocean. They could sail far and wide in the search of trade, plunder and settlement.

DAN ESCOTT

Norse settlers

The Norsemen first came to Scotland before 800AD; to the Isles of Shetland and Orkney, to Caithness in the north-east and to the Western Isles, Lewis and Skye. Those who came then were free-born, farmers driven from their old homes by the need for new lands. In South Shetland they found a settling place where they could sow their crops and tend their beasts. Here they could build their homes and rear their children. In the shadow of a crumbling broch, overlooking the shore, they constructed their first dwelling-houses. Few trees grew on Shetland, so the walls were of earth and turf packed tight and braced against the raking winds with a facing of drystone inside and out. What

above: Settlement at Jarlshof, from the air

Houses were oblong and had two doorways. One led to the living quarters where the fire burned in the central hearth and the other to where the cattle sheltered. A paved floor there made the byre easier to clean out, but where the people were, firm dry clay was a better surface for holding the fire's warmth.

timber could be found was used for the roof. Made from layers of turf and straw, it was carried on rafters supported by two long rows of posts planted firmly in the ground.

In the spring, the long narrow fields were turned with simple wooden ploughs tipped with stone, and the seed corn was scattered. In May, the new lambs were born and two more months saw the cutting of hay for the cattle's winter feed. The sheep spent their winters on the hillside grazings and their summer-shorn fleece was spun and woven to make warm woollen clothing. But it is not as bands of determined farmers seeking and, if necessary, seizing a better place to live that the Norsemen are remembered. Nor is it as settlers who brought their language and way of life to mix with the customs and everyday existence of the people already here, though these were the most important things they did in Scotland. In Lewis almost all the village names are Norse and in parts of Skye more than two-thirds. There is almost no other kind in the Northern Isles of Orkney and Shetland. The islands of what is now Scotland were settling grounds for the Norsemen, places where they came to find better living and where they would learn new ways. They married with local people and they prayed to Christ. Perhaps just to be on the safe side, they made vows to Thor too, against the dangers of the sea.

1 Odin, Thor, and Frey from a tapestry in Sweden
2 Viking's shoes found in York
3 Thor's hammer – a silver Viking brooch
4 Heads of Thor and Frey from the 9th century
5 Chess piece from the Isle of Lewis

Above all these things the Norsemen are remembered as those who came out of the sea in sleek longships, their scornful dragonhead prows riding high on the surf. Sea-steeds, keel-birds, reindeer of the surf, ravens of the wind, the Norsemen called their graceful craft that crunched on the shingle of undefended havens. Snatching their shields from the shipsides they surged up the beaches brandishing battle-axes, swords and spears; protected by their iron helmets and chain mail. These men had not come to settle but to plunder. These men were the Vikings.

Now there was a new enemy in the lands of the Picts and Scots, an enemy of all. They were raiders, pirates who came for silver and gold, slaves and cattle. They struck at monasteries, seizing precious and holy things, ripping the richly jewelled bindings from the lovely painted bibles, slaughtering all who barred their way. And where they had been they would come again, knowing that patient monks would rebind the books and craft yet again the silver and gold to grace the altars of their church, and restock and replant the fields.

All the land lived in dread, fearful that at any moment, in any place, the seaward sky would suddenly fill with the great sails of longships coursing swiftly in. Surprise was complete. These ships needed no more than a metre's depth to clear the keel and with a fair wind could easily better ten knots. They rode the heaving and chopping of the open sea just as surely as they skimmed the shelving of gentle beaches and all but the shallowest rivers. Nowhere was safe.

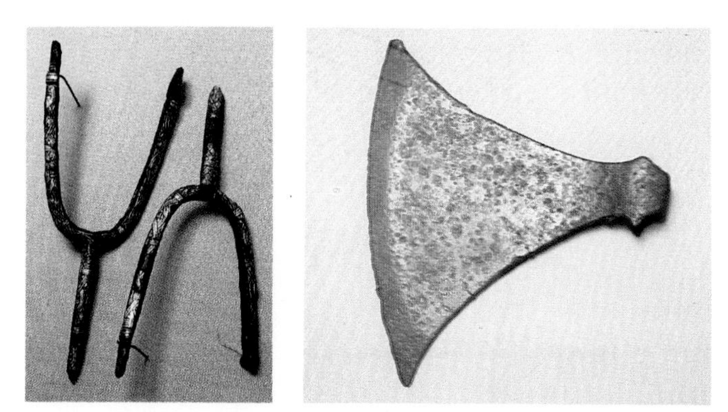

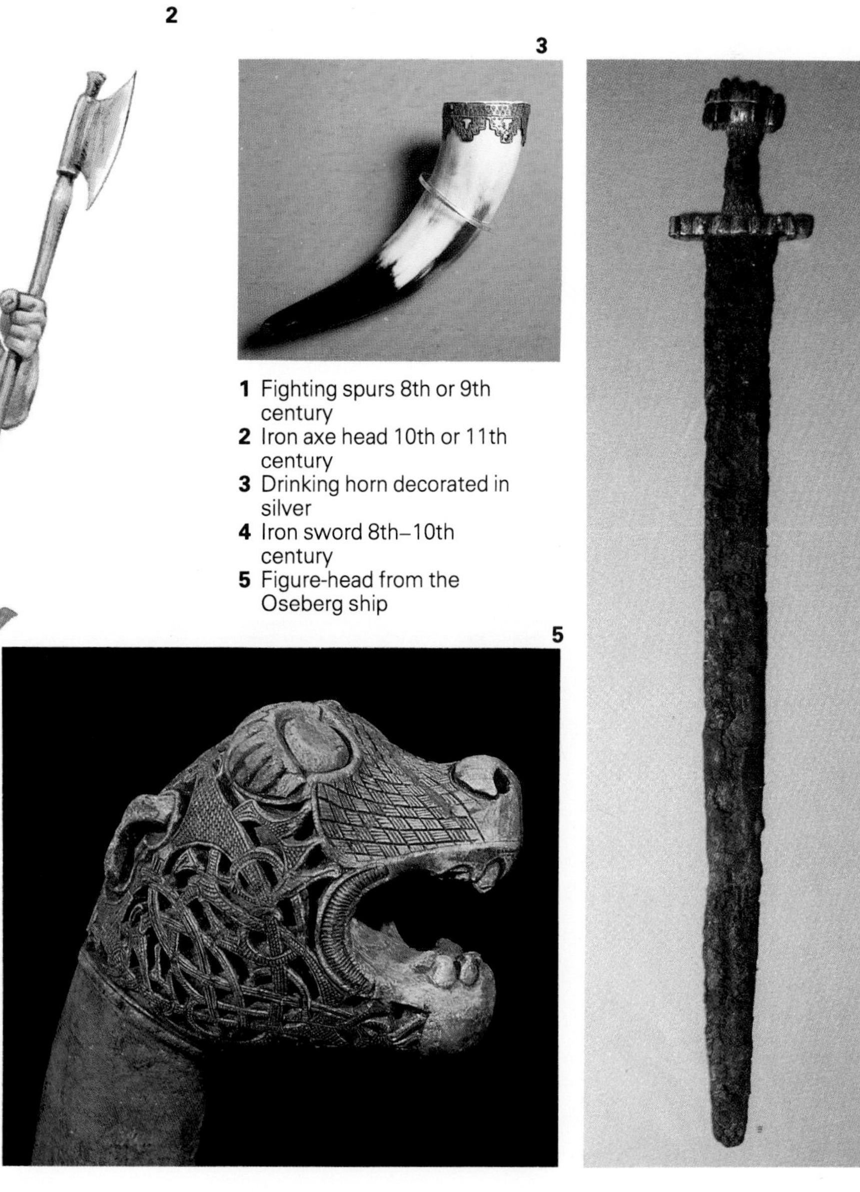

1 Fighting spurs 8th or 9th century
2 Iron axe head 10th or 11th century
3 Drinking horn decorated in silver
4 Iron sword 8th–10th century
5 Figure-head from the Oseberg ship

The raids on Iona

On the western isle to which St. Columba first brought his mission more than two centuries before, there still stood his monastery. There upon a gentle rise of grass and heather were closely huddled the abbot's house and monks' quarters, the scriptorium where lovely manuscripts were created and the little oratory in which earnest prayers were said, the barn, the mill and the byre. They looked out in peace over the narrow water to the low hills of Mull. This sacred place was the very heart of the Celtic Christian Church and here the faithful gathered to sing psalms under an open sky and against the sounds of wind and wave.

On a day of fair weather in the year of 795 their quiet devotion was shattered when square-sailed slender craft suddenly appeared and, with amazing speed, were grating on the sandy bay. The Vikings had come to Iona – to plunder and enslave, to kill and burn. And they struck again and again year after year until a terrible day in AD 825 when the com-

above: Martyr's Bay (Port Nan Mairtir) today

munity was massacred and a tiny cove earned the name Martyr's Bay. After that the sacred treasures were moved, some to Dunkeld in Perthshire and the rest, including the beautiful Four Gospels, to Kells in the north of Ireland.

And so began the long years of the Viking terror. For almost a century only bleak and stormy days, when sailing was impossible, passed without fear. But it was for much longer than this that the Norsemen remained in this land as settlers and rulers. No longer Scandinavians, they were now Christian people of the Isles and the northern mainland, Orcadians and Shetlanders, men of Caithness and the Hebrides. They had brought their art and metal craft, as beautiful as any their pirates had plundered. They had brought their wonderful ships and seamen's skill, their tools and their weapons, their language and their customs. And they had brought also, as a gift for all time, their own strain of talented and adventurous blood to mingle with that of Pict and Scot, Briton and Angle, in the making of a nation.

above: Viking warriors carved in stone

One Kingdom

In the year 841 a man called Kenneth mac Alpin became ruler of these Irish Scots in the Kingdom of Dal Riata. He was a warrior prince descended from Fergus Mor who first brought the tribe to Kintyre, and as with all leaders he held his kingdom by the might of his sword. He commanded obedience and tribute from the weak and resisted the challenge of others who thought their strength gave them rights too. And there would be many challenges. The bays and inlets of Argyll's rugged coast were open to the attacks of the Norse raiders from the west and north. To the east lay the power of the mighty Pictish kings.

Kenneth mac Alpin

In 843 Kenneth mac Alpin marched into Pictland with his war band brandishing long swords and wide spears, and carrying round shields of hide to fend off enemy weapons. He chose his time well. The Picts were weary from campaigning against the Norsemen and had little taste for battle. Partly because of this and perhaps because he had a claim to the crown of Pictland through his mother, Kenneth mac Alpin, Lord of Dal Riata, became King of the Picts.

left: Pictish cross – the 'Droslen Stone' 8th–9th century
below: Pictish stone from Aberlemno, Scotland

Two peoples united

The two peoples, the Scots in their western kingdom and the Picts in their much larger homeland found little difficulty in merging as one under their new leader. They already shared Christian beliefs, brought to them by St. Columba, and they had mingled and married together in the past. The ordinary people would have little enough idea about what was going on and would continue trying to stay alive and find their share of happiness. But what is very strange, is that their combined kingdoms, all the land between the ruins of the Antonine Wall in the south and the most northerly parts still held by the Norsemen, came to be known, not as Pictland but as Scotia, and the people – the Scots. They came also to speak Gaelic, the language of the Scots, and Pictish was forgotten. Those who had spoken it were soon to become a people of the past, their nickname, given to them by the Roman soldiers five centuries before, lost in history. Now there was a new united land in the grey north of Britain, a land called Scotland.

The Angles

He was an ambitious man, Kenneth mac Alpin, which in those days meant he wanted to be king of more than he already ruled. He wished to extend Scotia partly because of his ambition and partly because attacking is often the best way of defending. There were others who had unfriendly and ambitious eyes on his kingdom. In the south the Angles were strong and often tried to push their frontier north of the River Forth. The King of Scotia countered this by striking south. Six times he called his warrior host to the royal standard. Six times he crossed the Forth, south into Bernicia. Dynbaer on the east coast and Maelros where Eildon Hill North looks over the River Tweed were burned and looted. (To-day, we call them Dunbar and Melrose.) Under a sky dark with smoke the Scots pushed deep into the heartland of the Angles but were unable to subdue them. When, in AD 858, Kenneth mac Alpin was carried to his grave on Iona, the lands he had ruled had not been extended. But what matters more, he had held the new kingdom of the Scots for sixteen troubled years against attacks by Vikings from the Northern Isles and Britons from Strathclyde. The union of Pict and Scot would endure. The making of Scotland had begun.

Malcolm II

Two more centuries would pass and thirteen kings who ruled by the sword would, for the most part, die by it, before one would come to bring the peoples south of the Forth and Clyde under his rule. In 1005, the second king to bear the name Malcolm took the throne. Like those who went before him Malcolm II did not automatically become king. He had to be elected from a group of royal relatives. The group was called the derbfine and included anyone whose great-grandfather had held the crown. At least in theory the new monarch was meant to be a male of proper age and character to do the job required at the particular time. Malcolm obtained the throne by slaying his cousin King Kenneth III, which suggests that he had the strength anyway.

Malcolm II and courtiers

Kings of Scotland from 843–1097

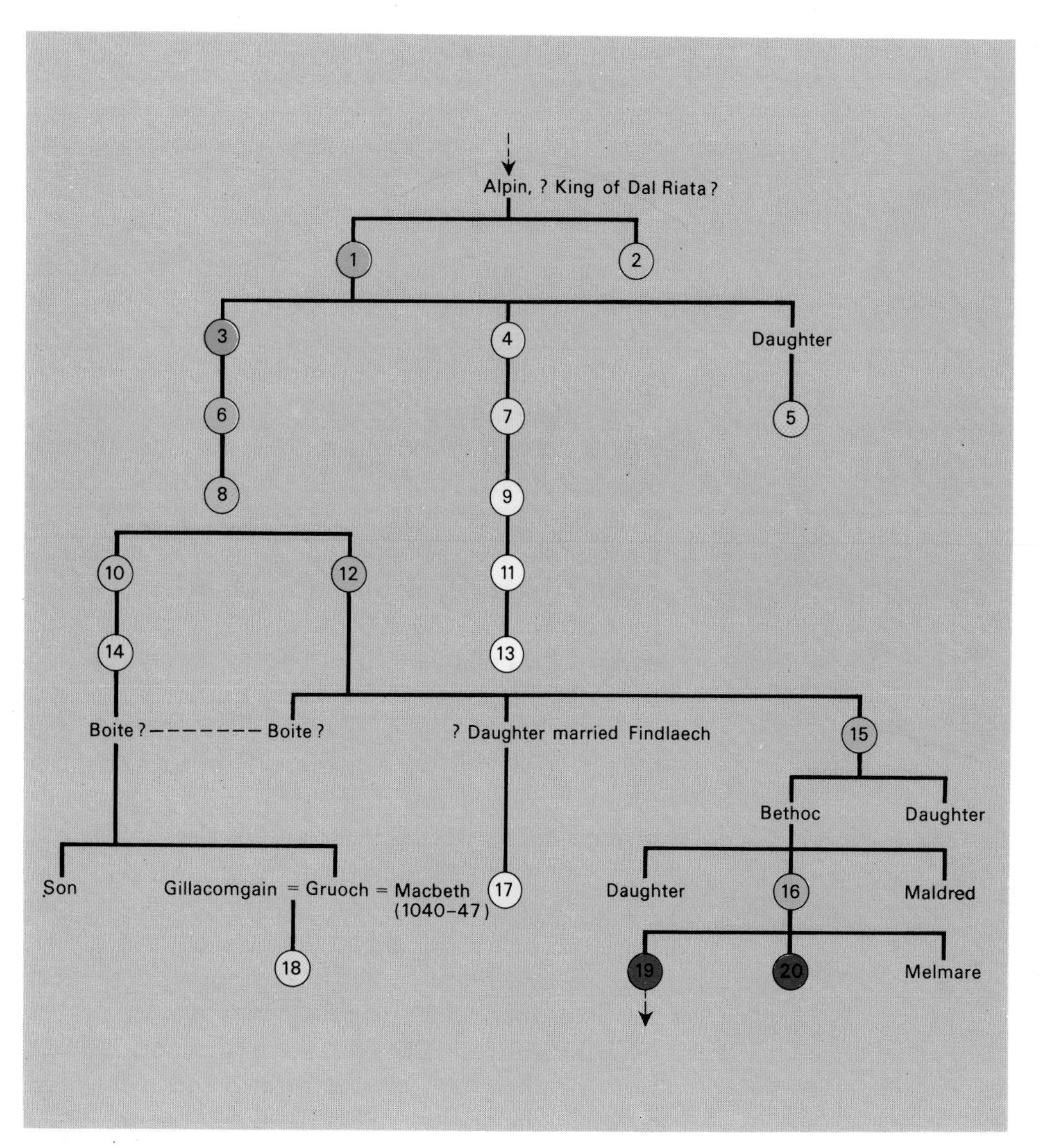

1 Kenneth MacAlpin (843–58)
2 Donald I (858–62)
3 Constantine I (862–77)
4 Aed (877–8)
5 Eochaid, Giric (878–89)
6 Donald II (889–900)
7 Constantine II (903–43)
8 Malcolm I (943–54)
9 Indulf (954–62)
10 Dubh (962–6)
11 Culen (966–71)
12 Kenneth II (971–95)
13 Constantine III (995–7)
14 Kenneth III (997–1005)
15 Malcolm II (1005–34)
16 Duncan I (1034–40)
17 Macbeth (1040–57)
18 Lulach (1057–58)
19 Malcolm III (1058–93)
20 Donald Bane (1093–4) (1094–7)

Macbeth married Gruoch, Gillacomgain's widow, and when he died in 1057 his stepson, Lulach (The Simple) reigned for 7 months and 3 days.

Malcolm III married twice. His eldest son by his first wife Ingibjorg (Duncan II) reigned for 6 months during 1094 when Donald Bane (his uncle) was deposed.

Donald Bane was deposed a second time in 1097 by Edgar (Malcolm III's fourth son by his second wife, Margaret) and was blinded and imprisoned for the rest of his life.

The king's rule

As king, he was head of state. He had about him a council of nobles and churchmen. He had definite powers too. The law was his law and his subjects kept the king's peace. He could demand a food rent and hospitality from his land owners. He could call upon his men for service in the defence of the realm.

But ruling was difficult, so much energy was spent in resisting attack or in travel. Sending messages was a slow process. And the whole thing was made even more difficult by the fact that, while the chiefs and landowners may have kept the king's command, the plain folk probably knew little about it. Many of them were still following their tribal ways, moving from place to place according to the season.

Battle of Carham

King Malcolm II had the same ambitions and needs as Kenneth mac Alpin. Scotia should be extended and he and his family should hold the throne. In 1018 he called the men of Scotia to his service and marched south into Bernicia, now the Lothians. He had assembled a mighty host and was aided by the Britons of Strathclyde under King Owen the Bald. He hacked his way south laying waste to the land and leaving a trail of burning and slaughter until at last he brought the Angles to battle at Carham on the banks of the Tweed. There he crushed their last resistance and seized for Scotia all the lands as far south as the Tweed where runs the present border of Scotland.

Scotland extended

In the same year, 1018, his ally King Owen died without a proper heir. King Malcolm was quick to help out the Britons, and placed his grandson Duncan on their throne. Now Briton and Angle had gathered with Pict and Scot under one leader. All of north Britain was subject to one King. Malcolm had proved to be of the right character for his time and extended his kingdom south to its present border. His ambition was fulfilled.

Duncan

Duncan was a very different character from his grandfather. He was headstrong and got off to a bad start. In securing the throne for him, his grandfather had slain a rival to the crown. Unfortunately for Duncan, the rival had a daughter who bore a son. In the Pictish way of things the crown passed through the mother's side of the family. To strengthen her son's claim she married a man of the north, an Earl of Moray who was himself of royal descent. His name was Macbeth.

Macbeth

The Northern Scots, who lived beyond the Mounth were like the Northern Picts. They did not care much for those who lived south of it and they certainly found if difficult to accept kings from there. Macbeth staked his claim. After six not very successful years as King the young Duncan decided to put down the rebellious Macbeth. It was a mistake. His march into Moray against Macbeth in 1040 resulted in his own defeat and death and in Macbeth taking the crown. He held it for seventeen years until another Malcolm, son of Duncan came north with allies from Northumbria. He first defeated Macbeth at Dunsinnan Hill, and drove him out of the Lothians and Strathclyde, perhaps even beyond the Mounth. Three years later he completed the conquest at Lumphanan in Aberdeenshire, slaying Macbeth and routing his supporters.

And so to the throne of Scotia in 1057 came Malcom III, King of Scots and with him the Royal House of Canmore which would rule over Scotland for more than two centuries.

below: Site of the battle of Dunsinnan Hill

inset: An eighteenth century interpretation of Shakespeare's *Macbeth*

Workection

The Coming of the Long Ships

Understand Your Work

The Norsemen

1 Find Scandanavia on your map and study its western coastline.
2 Where was the land farmed by the Norsemen?
3 What encouraged the Norsemen to look for new sources of food?
4 What was the change in their boats that enabled the Norsemen to master the oceans?
5 How were the seams between the planks of the Norse ships made watertight?
6 Were the planks nailed to the ribs of the boat?
7 What means of propulsion had these ships?
8 When did the Norsemen come to Scotland?
9 Look at the ships on page 65. How is a Viking ship different from a Roman trireme?

Norse Settlements

1 What kind of Norsemen first came to Scotland?
2 Where did they settle?
3 How were their houses constructed?
4 What was the inside of a Norse house like?
5 Why was paving used in the animals' quarters and bare clay for the people?
6 What means had the Norsemen for turning the soil?
7 How can we tell that a great many Norse people settled in islands like Orkney and Shetland and Lewis?
8 Were they Christians?
9 How is the house on page 66 different from the house on page 59?
10 Describe any 3 of the objects on page 69.

The Raiders

1 Not all Norsemen came to settle as farmers. What did the Vikings come for?
2 Why did they raid the monasteries?
3 Why were the longships able to ride in so close to the shore or up shallow rivers?
4 For how many years did they raid Iona?
5 What steps were taken by the monks to safeguard the treasures of the monastery from further attacks?
6 Why were bleak and stormy days a relief to the peoples of Scotland during the ninth century?
7 By what names did the Vikings call their longships?
8 What armour did they wear and what weapons did they carry?
9 What plunder did the Vikings seize?
10 Imagine you escaped from Martyr's Bay. Look at the picture on page 71 and say what happened.

One Kingdom

Kenneth mac Alpin

1 Who was Kenneth mac Alpin?
2 Why was the time he chose to attack the Picts right?
3 Had he any claim to the Pictish throne?
4 How well did the two peoples, Picts and Scots, mix together?
5 What was the language spoken by the united peoples?
6 Why was Kenneth mac Alpin anxious to extend his new kingdom?
7 Though he failed to make his kingdom larger what had he succeeded in doing?
8 Where was Kenneth mac Alpin buried?

Macolm II

1 What was the derbfine?
2 What type of person was thought fit to become monarch?
3 Who advised the king?
4 What were the royal powers?
5 Ruling a kingdom was made difficult by what problems?
6 Were the ordinary people loyal to the king?
7 How far did Malcom II extend the kingdom of the Scots?
8 Who challenged Malcolm II's grandson Duncan for the crown and why did he think he should be king?
9 How long did Macbeth rule?
10 What five peoples mixed to form the kingdom of the Scots?
11 Look at the picture on page 77. What was life like for such a family?

Use Your Imagination

1 How do you imagine it might have happened that the Norsemen first came upon Scotland and the rich plunder of its monasteries?

2 Why do you suppose the bow and stern of the Norse ships were high but the sides quite low? (Think about waves and pulling in nets.)

3 When Norse settlers arrived and met the local Picts they would speak in a quite different language. How do you think the Norsemen explained that they had come in peace and were not Viking raiders, without using words?

4 Why would it be wise of the Vikings when stealing the treasures of the monasteries to spare the people who made them?

5 Norsemen usually built their houses of wood? Why did they use turf and stone in some parts of the country?

6 Why did they settle in the same area as a broch had once stood?

7 Why do you think the Vikings carried their shields mounted on the gunwales (side rails) of their ships?

8 What special guard duties might Kenneth mac Alpin's navy have to perform?

9 Do you think the ordinary peasant in ancient Scotland knew who was King?
How would this affect the work of ruling the kingdom?

10 In what way do you think the derbfine was a better method of finding a new monarch than just taking the next in line? How might it be not so good?

Further Work

1 The Vikings told great tales of fighting and daring called sagas. You can write a different type of saga. Imagine that you are a member of a Norse expedition which has settled in Scotland. Describe the difficulties you had and the risks you took landing peacefully in another land and meeting local tribes, building houses and finding food, facing the first winter. It will be a tale of struggle and survival, not plunder and killing but it will be just as brave a story.

2 The keel made a great difference to the Norse ships. Your group can discover why. You will need to make a little boat like this

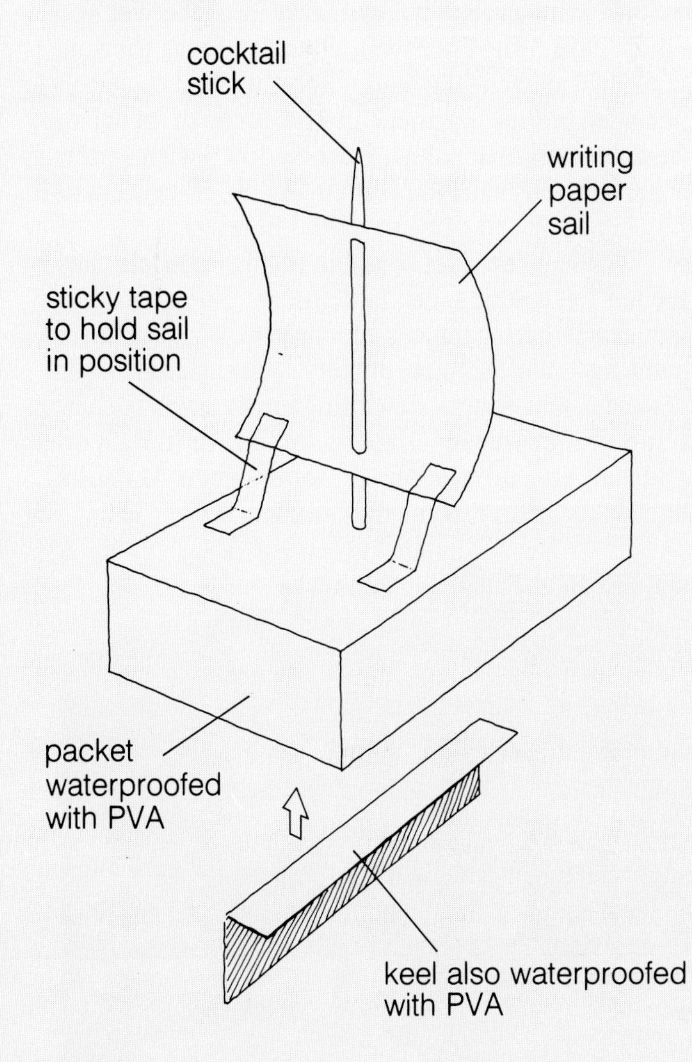

Float your boat without its keel in a basin of water. Blow gently on the sail from behind and from different angles, setting the sail with sticky tape. Now, dry your boat and stick on the keel.

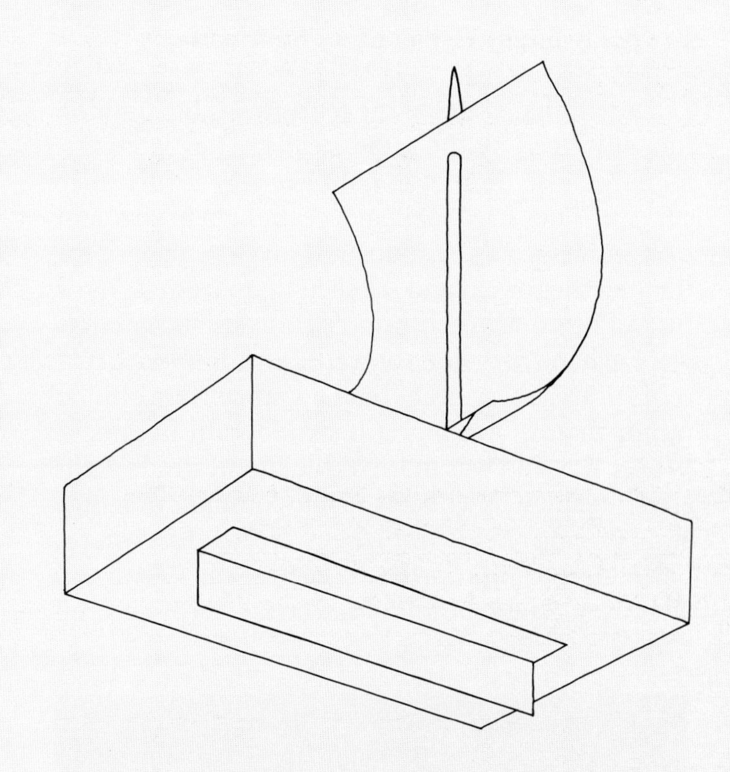

Repeat the sea trials and make notes of what you discover.

3 The voyages of the Norsemen were long and cold. You can write a poem telling how a Viking might have felt at sea in the winter. First think of the coldest day you can remember, the wind numbing your face. Can you feel the cold in your ears, nose, fingers, toes etc?
Now, you are a Viking all day sitting at the oar. What do you see, hear, feel, think, wish . . .?
Do not try to make the lines rhyme – just make them bitterly cold.
There is a very old poem translated from Anglo Saxon which is about this subject. It is called 'The Seafarer'. If you can find a copy, compare your work with it.

4 Burning houses were a common sight where the Vikings had been. You can make a picture of this scene.
First paint the background of land and sky. Then 'build' a low thatched cottage by sticking on paper 'stones' for the walls and straw for the roof.
When the cottage is ready, set it ablaze by pasting on bright red and yellow flames with dark billowing smoke. Finally add the Viking with battle axe and torch. He can be painted, cut out and pasted on beside the burning cottage.

5 Find out if Shakespeare's story of Macbeth is accurate? Why do you think he wrote the play the way he did?

Malcolm III and his Family

Everyday life in 11th century Scotland

Little had changed over the centuries. The common folk still lived by the same means. They were farmers because there was no other way for them to survive. They used tools and weapons of bronze and iron and bone. They spun and wove rough yarn for their clothes or cut and stitched them from skins or furs. They built their houses from what materials were to hand, drystone or wattle and daub with turf roofs or thatch. More often now, they were oblong rather than round but still shared with livestock. Where the land was more fertile, homesteads gathered together as villages using common grazings and sharing fields for their crops. Elsewhere, particularly in the north, the good earth was turned wherever it could be found and crofts were scattered wide.

Problems of farming

But there was a problem here and it was made worse by a growing population. More mouths to feed meant more fields for crops. The trouble was that in getting more fields, more pasture was being used up. This meant that only smaller herds could be supported and yet it was these herds that fertilized the land. Without fertilizer ground is soon exhausted and more fresh ground must be found. To make the whole thing even more difficult the oxen that pulled the plough required grazing too. Perhaps for this reason, horses began to be used in mixed teams with oxen. Horses eat oats. It was a hard life for the villagers, filled with uncertainty. Crops grew badly and harvests were often washed out in the wet and windy days. They ate well when food was there to be eaten and went without when they had to. Their diet was mainly oatmeal in the form of gruel or brose, porridge or cakes, washed down with water, or ale brewed from the barley. As much protein as they could afford came as salted herring.

These little places tried to produce all they needed to survive – but little more. They had part time craftsmen to make necessary tools – querns for grinding meal, crude pottery. Occasional visits from pedlars brought new things and variety to their living. Goods were exchanged for food or fuel, Scotland had still no system of money when Malcolm seized the throne from Macbeth in 1057.

In the village each homestead had its own small piece of ground on which stood the simple cottage and byre or barn. The villagers paid a food rent to their landlord and gave small services on his lands, perhaps a few days' work at times of ploughing, haymaking and harvest. Barley and oats were the crop mostly planted and they gave a poor enough return for all the patient labour. Only four ears of barley were harvested for each one planted, and one of the four had to be kept as the next year's seedcorn. It took a lot of work and a lot of ground to grow enough to live on and to meet the landlord's rent.

Forests had to be cut back and valuable pasture land turned under the plough. Teams of oxen, often eight strong, strained at the plough to break out new ground.

Christianity

But some things had changed. There was now a Christian message to believe in and to mix with myths and pagan memories. And there were simple churches of stone or timber round which religious people lived in simple houses of wattle and worked at carpenter's bench or blacksmith's forge. Grander monasteries had richer townships growing round them and no more Vikings to steal their treasures.

Language

North of the Forth and Clyde in Scotia the Gaelic spoken by the Scots was mixed with Pictish while, further south in Strathclyde, it was mixed with Ancient British. But to the east, between the Forth and Tweed, another language was now more loudly heard, spoken by the Angles who ruled the Lothians – a language called English. This was the language of Malcolm Canmore, King of Scots, learned in his early years while sheltering from Macbeth in England. Though the Scots of Dal Riata gave to land and race their name and royal dynasty, it was English that was to be the language of the kings and, one day, of all the people, Gaelic surviving only in the mountains and islands of the remote north-west.

This was the Celtic realm that Malcolm III came to rule, but, for all its troubles, it was Christian and it had a tradition, now more than two centuries old, of serving one King. This northern place had been a united land long before England and the countries of Western Europe.

above: Archbishop Stigant from the Bayeux Tapestry

Dryburgh Abbey

Melrose Abbey

below: A church of the period, at St. John's Point, Caithness

Malcolm III

Despite all his years of refuge in England and his liking for English ways and speech, King Malcolm was hardly on the throne (helped there by King Edward of England) before he had his war bands looting and burning south of the River Tweed. Five times or more he struck in Northumbria. He had personal ambitions to rule the North of England and many English people who had no ambitions to rule anyone, were slaughtered or enslaved as a result. Many Scots died too but England remained English.

English victories and defeats

Events did occur, however, nine years after he first came to the throne, that would change the history of all Britain and Malcolm may have played a part in them, though not the part he would have planned. It started simply enough with yet another invasion of Northumbria, not by Malcolm this time but by Harold Hardrada, King of Norway. Malcolm's wife was a relative of this king and perhaps for this reason, but more likely because of personal ambition, Malcolm may have given support to the invaders. If he did then he certainly did not help his own future hopes. When news of this invasion reached King Harold Godwinson of England he marched quickly north to meet and defeat the intruders at Stamford Bridge. No sooner was the fighting over than alarming news reached him from the south coast. At once his army was on the march again with little time for rest. The year was 1066 and King Harold was pushing south with all speed to Hastings. He was roundly defeated by the new invaders, the men of William the Conqueror, Duke of Normandy, only eighteen days after repelling the Norwegians.

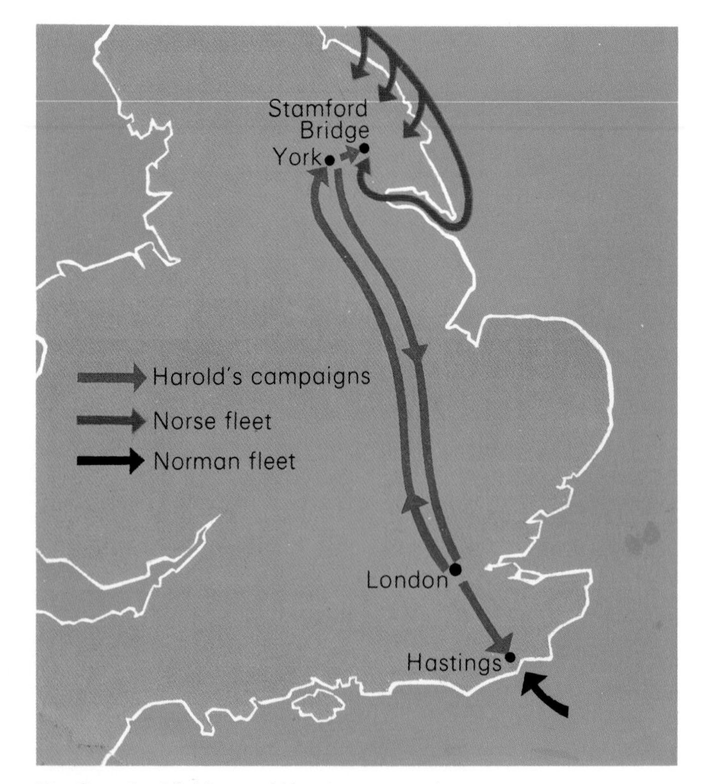

The Stamford Bridge and Hastings campaigns

The Normans

The Normans were an amazing people. Descended from Viking settlers of an earlier age (their name means North Men), their homeland was in France amongst the rolling green countryside on either bank of the River Seine where it empties into the English Channel. In not much more than a century this little dairy-farming community became the masters of Sicily, southern Italy and most of Britain; equals of the Kings of France in power and importance.

below: Site of the battle of Hastings, Battle in Sussex
bottom: Sections of the Bayeux Tapestry

Edgar

For his first year or two in England, William had little time for Malcolm and his misty quarrelsome kingdom of the North. But in 1068 something did happen because of his conquest. Edgar Atheling last of King Alfred's line and who had a claim to England's crown, sought refuge from the Normans with the King of Scots. He brought with him his sister Margaret. By 1071 she had become Malcolm's second wife, married probably in Dunfermline Priory.

Malcolm confronts William the Conqueror

Through his marriage Malcolm found a claim to the throne of England. William, knowing the kind of man who ruled the northern kingdom, was determined to put an end to any new ambitions Malcolm might be having. He marched north and, just as Agricola had done a thousand years before, he sent his fleet up the eastern edge of Scotland to threaten the Scots and support his troops. Up through the Lothians pressed the great column, a swaying forest of upthrust lances with pennants flying, the air filled with the heavy beat of hoof and foot on the hard-packed road. No defending army barred their way. They pushed on to the River Forth at Stirling where horse and man waded through the shallow water to strike north-east to Abernethy and the Firth of Tay. There in the sight of the Norman fleet William drew up his army in battle order. The Normans had perfected fighting on horseback. They had special saddles and stirrups which allowed them to wield their weapons and shields while still controlling their horses. They had also developed the use of the long-bow in war. They were too much for Malcolm. Rather than risk defeat which seemed certain, he met with William and sought his mercy, promising to be faithful and loyal in the future. It suited Malcolm to pay homage then and avoid battle and it did not stop him attacking England later, but it certainly made problems for the Scots in the years to come. The idea that an English king had a right to rule the Scots led to centuries of bloodshed and bitter fighting.

Broken peace

The loyalty shown by King Malcolm to his Norman overlord lasted seven years and then once more his war bands burned and looted the villages of Northumbria. Again the Normans marched north, and again Malcolm knelt before their leader, only this time it was William's son Robert and the place was Falkirk. And it went on like this to the end: looting and wasting, burning and merciless slaughter, followed by more promises of peace and loyalty. Malcolm never did gain Northumbria for the Scottish crown and he always seemed more interested in plunder and personal profit rather than conquest. In the end he died on yet another raid in the luckless and wasted countryside of Northumbria. He was slain, perhaps murdered, outside Alnwick, on the 13th November 1093, and his queen, who had been ill for some time, died three days later. Edward, their eldest son who had been wounded with his father, died the day before his mother.

Queen Margaret

Queen Margaret had brought more to the land of the Scots than a claim to an English throne. She was a clever and energetic woman devoted to her Church. Though she was Anglo-Hungarian by birth and blood she liked the ways of the Normans. She brought to her new homeland spiced meats and French wines, lovely tapestries and rich clothes, dancing and the singing of ballads. She lived true to her beliefs giving most generously to the poor, building a beautiful Church at Dumfermline and filling it with lovely and precious things. She taught the priests to live simply and without wealth, giving their whole lives to their Christian belief, helping the needy, comforting the sick and troubled. She worked endlessly to make the Church of the Scots become more like the Church in Rome. Queen Margaret's life of charity and kindly example, her high learning and Christian service so impressed the rough and ambitious Malcolm that he supported his wife's good works. He allowed his wealth to be given away to the poor and Church alike. On one occasion he knelt beside her as she washed the feet of a beggar. On another, filled his royal hall with three hundred needy subjects so that they might be fed. Throughout her reign Margaret brought a softness to his harsh kingdom of the north and in the passing of time was made the Saint that, during her life, many common folk had known her to be.

1 Nineteenth century painting of Queen Margaret and Malcolm
2 Round arch in Queen Margaret's chapel, Edinburgh
3 Modern window in Queen Margaret's chapel, Edinburgh
4 Queen Margaret's chapel, Edinburgh
5 Bible, commissioned by Queen Margaret, now in Oxford
page opposite: Dunfermline Abbey, built by Margaret and extended by her son, David I.

Threat from the north

Not everyone felt devoted to this queen and her Norman ways. When she and Malcolm and their eldest son Edward, heir to the throne, all died in four days there was a change of mood. South from the grey Hebrides came Donald Bain who claimed the crown by Pictish rights. He was supported by the Northern Scots who disliked the English. He came as a warrior chief to seize what he said was his rightful throne and to expel the Anglo-Norman members of the Royal Court and the Church, the mail-clad knights, the singers of ballads and men of trade. Even the dead queen had to be secretly removed from her chapel on Edinburgh's castle rock. Under cover of thick fog and darkness her sons carried her body across Queensferry, which she herself had provided for pilgrims from the Lothians travelling to Dunfermline Abbey where her body was now being taken for safety. And so began again the hating and the killing as, sword in hand, ambitious men argued their claims to the Scottish throne, fighting, even murdering, any others who thought they too had some right to rule.

In three years the crown changed heads three times – from Donald III by battle to Duncan II, by murder back again to Donald III, and by battle to Edgar, son of Margaret and Malcolm. Both Duncan and Edgar were helped by English armies and were not really free kings. They owed rather too much to William Rufus, the Conqueror's son, now King of England.

Sons of Malcolm III

Edgar reigned for nine years and was a man of peace, not at all like his father. He had little interest in the part of his kingdom north of the Forth and Clyde, the part called Scotia, with its grey mountains and misty islands. When the men of the Western Isles rose in rebellion against their Norse overlords it was Magnus Bareleg, King of Norway who put down the revolt and then had little trouble in keeping the islands for himself – little trouble from Edgar that is. The local chiefs had developed a taste for independence and continued to rebel.

Edgar was content to rule the mainland but not now from Dunfermline. He made his royal home at Edinburgh Castle and there was peace with England.

When he died in 1107 Edgar left the care of his kingdom to his two brothers, Alexander to rule the north and David, Strathclyde and the Lothians. But only Alexander was to be king. David would rule under his older brother.

These three brothers who held and shared the Scottish crown for sixty years were only half Scots. Their mother, the saintly Queen Margaret, gave them an English half and some of her devotion to the Church. The long periods they had spent in England taught them the Norman ways. Donald Bane their uncle and fierce Scot of the north, had been the last of the Celtic Kings.

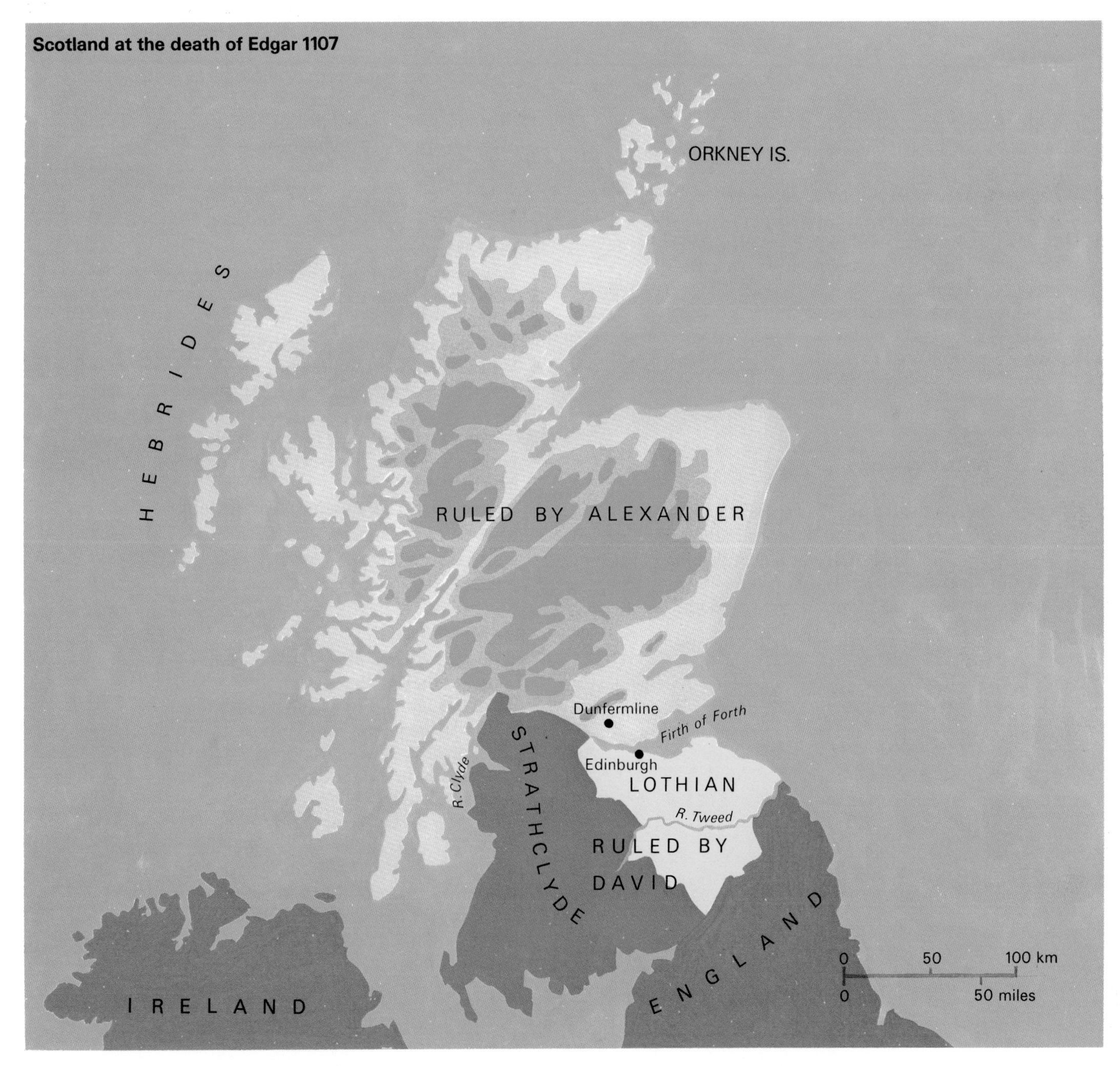

Worksection

Malcolm III

Understand Your Work

Every day life in 11th Century Scotland

1 What was the main occupation of the Scottish people in the 11th Century?
2 What metals were in common use?
3 From what were clothes made?
4 How were the houses constructed?
5 Why were the crofts scattered and not gathered in villages?
6 Who made the necessary tools and pottery?
7 Who supplied goods not made in the village and how were these paid for?
8 What were the usual foodstuffs?

The Village

1 What did a homestead consist of?
2 How was rent paid for the land?
3 What crops were most commonly grown?
4 Why were the forests being cut back?
5 How many oxen were used to pull the plough?
6 What was happening because pasture was used for crops?
7 How did horses help?
8 In what forms was oatmeal eaten?
9 Imagine you are in the picture on page 83. Describe your village.

Christianity and Language

1 Where did the people worship?
2 What was the main language they spoke?
3 What was the new language to be heard in the Lothians?
4 What language did King Malcolm III speak in his court?
5 Where did Malcolm learn this language?
6 How long had Scotland been a united kingdom?

Malcolm III

1 Did Malcolm's time in England make him more friendly towards it?
2 Who suffered when kings tried to seize more land?
3 King Harold Godwinson of England faced two invaders within three weeks. Who were they?
4 Where did the Normans come from?
5 How did Malcolm get a claim to England's throne?
6 What happened when William marched against Malcolm III?
7 What idea did Malcolm's promises give to kings of England?
8 How well did Malcolm keep his promises to William?
9 Was Malcolm successful in his attempts to extend Scotland further south?
10 What happened to the royal family of Malcolm from 13th to 16th November 1093?
11 Describe what is happening in the scenes from the Bayeux Tapestry on pages 86 & 87.

Queen Margaret

1 What was Queen Margaret's great interest?
2 Was she a Norman?
3 What new ideas did she bring to the royal court?
4 How did she encourage the priests to live?
5 Where did she build her church?
6 How did Margaret influence her husband Malcolm III?
7 Where was the ferry she provided for the pilgrims travelling between the Lothians and Dumfermline?
8 How was Queen Margaret's great devotion to her religion later rewarded?
9 Can you decorate a manuscript in the style of picture 5 on page 90?

After Malcolm III

1 Who were Queen Margaret's enemies?
2 Why did they dislike her?
3 What did Donald Bane come south to do?
4 Why was the Queen's body moved from Edinburgh to Dumfermline?
5 How was King Edgar different from those who held the throne before him?
6 What part of the country did he show little interest in?
7 How did Edgar divide the kingdom between his brothers?
8 Who was the last of the Celtic kings of Scotland?
9 Compare the map on page 93 with a modern map. Describe the territorial borders using modern names of places, rivers, etc.

Use Your Imagination

1 How did the fact that horses eat oats make it a good idea to use them instead of oxen for ploughing when pasture was becoming scarce?

2 Why do you think more of the houses were now oblong rather than round?

3 Why was it that William the Conqueror decided to march against Malcolm when news of his wedding to Margaret reached William?

4 What do you suppose the common rough Celt thought of the fine pretty clothes, dancing and music which Margaret brought to the royal court?

5 Why did Queen Margaret want priests to live simply and without wealth?

6 Can you imagine why the common folk thought their Queen to be a saint?

7 More is known about the kind of houses people lived in than about the ships they used. Why do you think this is so?

Further Work

1 Often the only way to defeat forces who held a strong position is to get them to move out of it. Can you think of any tactics or tricks you might use to do this? Find out what happened to King Harold and his army at the Battle of Hastings, where they held a strong position on Senlac Hill.

2 Kings always risked rebellions among their subjects usually led by someone who wanted to be king. What steps do you think you might take to discourage people from rebellion and encourage them to be loyal.

3 Paint a picture showing the colourful things of beauty and clothes brought to the royal court by Queen Margaret showing people dancing and musicians playing. If you like you could have a window where two Scots peasants are looking in – amazed! You could add a caption showing what they are saying. (See picture below.)

4 Try to visit Dumfermline and see the remains of Queen Margaret's church there. Find out when she was made a saint and where she and King Malcolm III are buried.